THEODORE M. BENDITT

Law as Rule and Principle

PROBLEMS OF LEGAL PHILOSOPHY

Stanford University Press, Stanford, California

1978

Stanford University Press
Stanford, California
© 1978 by the Board of Trustees of the
Leland Stanford Junior University
Printed in the United States of America
ISBN 0-8047-0963-7   LC 77-89180

To my mother

Preface

The field of legal philosophy has become considerably richer during the past two decades. Much of the attention has been focused on moral and other philosophical problems connected with law, but there has also been considerable interest in legal theory—philosophical theories about what might grandly be called the nature of law. The problems taken up in this book fall largely into the latter area.

The chapters of the book divide into three groups. The first two chapters consist of an exposition and critique of legal realism. The next three chapters consist of some work in the area of contemporary legal theory, including a discussion of what a theory of law is, a critique of Professor Ronald Dworkin's recent and influential writings, and a defense of a natural law position that I call the functional theory of law. The final three chapters are independent essays that are related to themes in earlier parts of the book and concern matters of general interest in legal philosophy: whether a legal system necessarily employs coercive sanctions, what sorts of obligations there are with respect to the law, and whether legal rights and duties are logically correlated.

Though this book is not intended as an introduction to legal philosophy, a good bit of the first few chapters was written with the student very much in mind. This accounts to a great extent for the amount of space devoted to legal realism, which in my experience students find interesting and plausible. Perhaps others also will find the chapters on realism useful, since some of the material later in the book recalls that earlier discussion.

I began the work that resulted in this book while I held a fellowship from the National Endowment for the Humanities in 1974–75. I wish to thank the Endowment for its support.

I would like to thank Robert Audi, David Braybrooke, Richard Bronaugh, and James Rachels for providing comments on various chapters.

Chapter 2 is a revised version of my article "Legal Theory and Rules of Law," *Western Ontario Law Review*, 13 (1974), and Chapter 5 is a revision of my article "A Functional Theory of Law," *Western Ontario Law Review*, 14 (1975). I thank the editor for permission to use the material contained in those articles.

I would like to acknowledge the fine editing of Barbara E. Mnookin, Associate Editor of Stanford University Press. Anne S. Benditt also provided able editorial assistance, and her efforts in the preparation of the manuscript were magnificent.

T.M.B.

Contents

Law as Rule and Principle

1

Legal Realism

Judges ascertain and apply the law. This is what almost everyone would suppose, and legal writers as far apart in their views of law as Sir William Blackstone and Jeremy Bentham have shared at least this opinion. Blackstone thought that anything that is properly thought of as human law is in accordance with the law of nature, which is dictated by God and "is binding over all the globe, in all countries, and at all times."[1] A judge's task, thought Blackstone, is to ascertain what this law is and to apply it to the case before him. Judges in no sense make the law. Bentham, on the other hand, maintained that a good deal of law is in fact made by judges, though he thought that it should not be. All law that regulates the behavior of man in society, he held, is of human creation, and it should all be made by the legislature in accordance with the principle of utility. So according to Bentham, too, judges are to find the law—in legislative enactments only—and not make it.[2]

In agreement with Bentham and against Blackstone the group of legal writers called American legal realists maintain that judges do in fact make law. But against Bentham they maintain that judges should take a hand in making law, and against both Bentham and Blackstone they maintain that judges must be makers of law—and by "must" is meant that judges necessarily make law, that this is intrinsic to the very process or activity of judging. As one would expect, these contentions of the legal realists are not completely isolated from larger considerations about the nature of law. The realists (or some of them, at any rate) maintain that by approaching the study of law from the direction of the judicial process, we can gain insights that will yield a view of law quite different from the picture presented or implied by such writers as Blackstone and Bentham.

THE DEDUCTIVE MODEL OF LEGAL REASONING

One of the main aims of the realists is to expose what they see as a mistaken and indeed simpleminded picture of legal reasoning. In this picture the task of a judge is to find the law and apply it to the particular circumstances of a case he is judging. In this model the applicable rule of law is the major premise of a given piece of legal reasoning, the relevant facts of the case constitute the minor premise, and the conclusion (the decision that the judge is to make) is arrived at by a straightforward and airtight piece of deductive reasoning. This may be called the deductive model of legal reasoning. All aspects of this picture of legal reasoning, as well as certain views of law associated with it, have been attacked by some realist or other.

Some of the classical versions of natural law theory have been seen by many realists as the culprits in producing the picture of judicial reasoning just outlined. An example of such a natural law theory is Blackstone's. Blackstone, as we have seen, believed there exist laws that are not created by human beings but that are binding on them. These laws are of divine origin and are immutable, eternal, and perfect. In deciding cases judges are attempting to discover what these laws are and to apply them correctly to the cases that come before them. (This is not the entirety of Blackstone's view, but it is the part that most concerns realists.) The realists believe that such a view of law is silly ("transcendental nonsense"); laws, they say, are products of human creation, not ideal entities drawn up in heaven. If the realists are correct in their rejection of such natural law views (we will not pursue this here), then one picture of law that is naturally associated with the suspect model of judicial reasoning is mistaken, and support for the model is to that extent undermined. If judges can be said to find or discover the law at all, it is certainly not by a process in which pure reasoning reveals laws that can be plugged into simple syllogisms to yield unequivocal results. To pretend that this is how judges operate is to do violence to the facts; either it is to exhibit ignorance of the actual workings of the judicial process, or else it is to hold on to the results of *a priori* thinking in the face of the facts.

We can see here the kind of methodology employed by the realists. We are not to theorize about law by the exercise of *a priori* thinking that does not come to terms with the facts, and we are not to impose our preconceived ideas on the facts. We are instead to *see* what the facts are. If we want to know what legal reasoning is like, we must see how judges actually reason.

What is it that we see when we look at the actual workings of the judicial process? What we see first of all, say the realists, is that rules of law do not play the kind of central role in legal reasoning that is claimed by the deductive model. For it is a notorious and noteworthy fact that different judges, employing their own reasoning processes, reach different results in similar cases and even in the very same case. Consider, as an example, the following partially hypothetical case given by Jerome Frank in *Law and the Modern Mind*. The Blue & Gray Taxi Co., a Kentucky corporation, contracted with a railroad to have the exclusive privilege of soliciting taxi business on and adjacent to the railroad's depot. Purple Taxi Co., a rival, ignored this contract and solicited business around the depot. Blue & Gray wanted to prevent such activity by Purple. Since both Blue & Gray and Purple were Kentucky corporations, suit would have to be brought in the state courts rather than in the Federal District Court in Kentucky. But Blue & Gray wanted to bring suit in the Federal court because the Kentucky courts held such contracts invalid under Kentucky law, whereas the Federal court would very likely hold them to be valid under Kentucky law. So Blue & Gray reincorporated in Tennessee, dissolved the Kentucky corporation, sued in the Federal court, and won.[3]

Given occurrences like this, it is apparent, say the realists, that there are no binding legal rules at work in the process of judicial reasoning, for if there were we would not see this diversity of judicial opinion in the same and similar cases. Rules do not determine outcomes, for there may be no unequivocal rules available. Alternatively, there may be conflicting rules that apply to the facts of a case, so that "the rules" do not yield an unequivocal result. Rather, a judge must decide which rules to apply, and this is done in an act of judicial reasoning in which there are no *other* rules telling the judge which rule to apply. The upshot is that judges, far from being bound by rules, are free either to choose among rules where more than one applies—perhaps not arbitrarily, but by their own lights—or to decide cases on their own where there are no applicable rules at all. Indeed, the realists tell us, when we look closely at the actual operation of the judicial system, keeping points like this in mind, we see that judges are free to reach any result in a case that they wish to reach; they are not bound at all, by rules or anything else. It might appear that when a legislature has enacted statutes, judges are bound by the rules formulated by these statutes. But, say the realists, the reality of things differs from the appearance—for since judges have the last word in the interpretation of statutes, they are not in fact bound by any such rules to reach one decision rather than another.

What is developing, via the foregoing considerations, is the picture of a judge as an independent operative, perhaps consulting but not in reality bound by rules in arriving at his decisions. This picture looks even more accurate, realists point out, when we become acquainted with the way in which judges actually arrive at their decisions. The deductive model makes it look as if all that judges must do is get clear about the facts of the case and then simply look through the law books for a rule that, when applied to the facts, will yield an unequivocal result. But what actually happens (though only a few judges might be candid enough to admit it) is that after having surveyed the facts and read the briefs and the authorities, a judge gets an intuition—a hunch—about what the decision should be. This is usually all the "reasoning" there is as far as a judge's arriving at a decision is concerned. Of course, in writing his opinion a judge will dress it up, will provide an "apologia" for his decision, a "rationalization," an "effusion . . .

by which that decree is explained or excused."⁴ He will do this in order to make his decision acceptable by representing it as being in accordance with the official doctrine—i.e. with the deductive model—though the reality is not (usually) in accordance with that model.

All of the foregoing contentions deployed by realists against the deductive model are part of a general skepticism about the role that the deductive model accords to rules in the judicial process. Realists are also skeptical about what they see as a simpleminded conception of the role played by facts. In the deductive model a judge first discerns the facts and then finds the applicable rule; and statements expressing the facts constitute the minor premise in legal reasoning. But this view of the role of facts is also wrong-headed, according to Frank:

> The judge, in arriving at his hunch, does not nicely separate his belief as to the "facts" and his conclusion as to the "law"; his general hunch is more integral and composite, and affects his report—both to himself and to the public—concerning the facts. Only a superficial thinker will assume that the facts as they occurred and as they later appear to the judge (and as he reports them) will invariably—or indeed often—correspond. The judge's decision is determined by a hunch arrived at long after the event on the basis of his reaction to fallible testimony.⁵

The deductive model presupposes that the determination of the facts can be separated from the determination of what rules are to be applied to the facts. *"But these two parts of judging are usually not separated, but intertwined.* Generally it is only after a man makes up his mind, that he attempts, and then artificially, to separate these two operations."⁶

JOHN CHIPMAN GRAY'S THEORY OF LAW

The deductive model, as an account of how judicial reasoning works, has thus been thoroughly discredited, according to the realists: the role of factual determinations, of determinations of what the rules of law are, and of reasoning from rules and facts to decisions in particular cases have all been scored. We may leave to one side the criticism of the official theory of the role of facts and focus on the other criticisms. In particular, we will look at one theory of law that accepts the foregoing criticisms of the role of rules in judicial decision making. This is the legal theory of John Chipman Gray, as set forth in his book *The Nature and Sources of the Law*, written in 1909.[7] Gray is not, strictly speaking, a legal realist; but the central position that his theory assigns to courts and judges in a legal system gives it a close affinity to legal realism. He is sometimes looked on as a forerunner of realism, though some writers characterize him as a realist. According to Gray,

[T]he law of the State or of any organized body of men is composed of the rules which the courts, that is, the judicial organs of that body, lay down for the determination of legal rights and duties. The difference in this matter between contending schools of Jurisprudence arises largely from not distinguishing between the Law and the Sources of the Law.[8]

This compact statement of Gray's account of law requires explanation. First of all, judicial reasoning, according to Gray, is deductive in form: judges apply legal rules to facts and logically draw a conclusion that they give as the decision of the case. But these rules do not preexist the judicial decision: they do not exist eternally in heaven for all time, to be discovered by the judge in an act of *a priori* thinking; they are not even found in legislation; rather, they are made by judges. Hence, judges do apply rules, but only those that they themselves make. The judge is indeed the very central figure in the legal system. All law is judge-made law.

In support of this view Gray offers some of the arguments that have been brought out previously. In particular he offers the following. First, any view of law (such as a natural law theory like Blackstone's) contending that judges are discoverers and not makers of the law, and implying that judges may be mistaken in saying what the law is, is without practical significance. A judge is not, Gray says, an investigator in the legal sphere in the way that Newton was in the physical:

[T]he difference between the judges and Sir Isaac is that a mistake by Sir Isaac in calculating the orbit of the earth would not send it spinning around the sun with an increased velocity; his answer to the problem would be simply wrong; while if the judges, in investigating the reasons on which the Law should be based, come to a wrong result, and give forth a rule which is discordant with the eternal verities, it is none the less Law. The planet can safely neglect Sir Isaac Newton, but the inhabitants thereof have got to obey the assumed pernicious and immoral rules which the courts are laying down, or they will be handed over to the sheriff.[9]

Second, the law is what the courts say it is and not what the legislature's statutes say it is, for judges have the last word in interpreting statutes. "[F]or, after all, it is only words that the legislature utters; it is for the courts to say what those words mean; that is, it is for them to interpret legislative acts."[10] Again: "[S]tatutes do not interpret themselves; their meaning is declared by the courts, and *it is with the meaning declared by the courts, and with no other meaning, that they are imposed on the community as Law.* . . . [T]he power of the judges over the statutes is very great."[11] Gray sums up his position with the following passage from the celebrated English prelate Bishop Benjamin Hoadly (1676–1761): "Whoever hath an *absolute authority* to interpret any written or spoken laws, it is *he* who is truly the *Law-giver* to all intents and purposes, and not the person who first wrote or spoke them."[12] And likewise, says Gray, "whoever hath an absolute authority not only to interpret the Law, but to say what the Law is, is truly the Law-giver."[13]

Two important consequences of Gray's views as so far set out, which he explicitly notes, should be indicated. First, for the same reasons that statutes are not law, neither are prior judicial rulings, even if they are the rulings of the same court and even of the same judge. After all, judicial precedents are only words, written in the past by some judge, and it is only as currently interpreted that they have impact on the community. Second, that the courts are making law, and not merely stating or discovering it, means that they "have been constantly in the practice of applying in the decision of controversies, rules which were not in existence and were, therefore, not knowable by the parties when the causes of controversy occurred. . . . [C]ourts are constantly making *ex post facto* Law."[14] With few exceptions, Gray acknowledges, all law is retroactive; and he is candid enough to point out that "the Law of which a man has no knowledge is the same to him as if it did not exist."[15] This leads to Gray's conception of the function of judges. Their function, he says, "is not mainly to declare the Law, but to maintain the peace by deciding controversies,"[16] which is to say, by determining the legal rights and duties of the parties.[17] When a controversy comes before a judge, he must decide the case; he lays down a rule that settles the rights and duties of the parties; "that rule is the Law, and yet the rights and duties of the parties were not known by them. That is the way the parties are treated and have to be treated by the courts."[18]

If statutes and precedents are not law, what are they? Gray distinguishes between the law and the sources of the law. When judges formulate rules of law, they do not do so arbitrarily; they look to certain authoritative sources for guidance on what rules should be laid down. The sources from which judges draw their general rules are statutes, judicial precedents, opinions of experts, customs, and principles of morality and public policy.[19] We need not go into these at any length, but three of Gray's comments are worth noting. First, he tells us, some kinds of authoritative or expert materials must almost by necessity be among the sources of law. Legislation does not cover all of the areas of possible controversy that courts may be called on to deal with, and the work of courts would be quite unmanageable if they were to rethink each issue and not take some things as established.[20] Second, to say that judges make law means not only that they formulate the rules for their decisions in particular cases, but also that they thereby create precedents, sources of law in future cases.[21] Third, since morality is a source of law, the principles of morality are an appropriate subject of jurisprudential investigation.[22] The principles Gray has in mind here, we should note, are the true principles of morality and not the opinions of the community on questions of morality, for morality is different from custom as a source of law.[23] However, that morality is a source of law does not mean, he insists, that the law is anything other than what the court says it is.

Now, if certain sources of law are authoritative, where do they get their authority? What limits judges to the authoritative sources?

Gray's answers to these questions involve his views on the place of the law in the larger political framework, i.e. on the connection between the law and the state. If the state is identified with the rulers of a society—the sovereign, the legislature, or something or someone else—then we can see, Gray says, that not all law emanates from the state.[24] Statutory law is at best part of the law, and in any event, by his contention, the statutes themselves cannot be taken as laws since they will be applied only as interpreted by the judiciary. But if the law and the state are different, what is the state? And what is its connection with law and with the judicial organs in society? The state, Gray holds, is an artificial person, a personified abstraction, which is created in order to give coherence and continuity to the activities of the individuals occupying those offices that, as a group, exist to protect and advance human interests.[25] The state is created by, and its continued existence depends on, the rulers of the society. These individuals, the real rulers of a society, wield the power in society, but they "are undiscoverable. They are the persons who dominate over the wills of their fellows."[26] They may have official positions, but they need not. These rulers, whose power is the power of the state, determine what the authority of the legislature, judiciary, and administrative organs shall be, for, Gray says, these organs function at the sufferance of the rulers.

Nevertheless, as we have seen, Gray holds that the law is made up of the rules for decision laid down by courts. And courts determine, he says, the rights and duties of citizens and even of the state itself.[27] How does this fit in with his account of the state and its relation to the judicial organs? The power of the judges is not, in his view, absolute; they have only such power as the state gives them.[28] The state limits the power of the courts by "indicating the sources from which they are to derive the rules which make up the Law."[29] But now the question arises: "Who is to determine whether the judges are acting within these limits?"[30] Gray answers:

In all the less important matters, the rulers intrust the determination of this question to the judges themselves; thus the judges are allowed to say what are the details of the organization of a State and the distribution of its powers among its organs; but, on the most vital matters, the rulers themselves determine what the organization of the body is and within what limits its organs shall work; and the acts and declarations of persons, being its organs, which are inconsistent with the very nature of the organization, are not acts and declarations of the State—are not its Law.[31]

RULE NIHILISM

Most of what Gray says about law appeals to realists. But Gray does view laws as rules—rules that are made by judges, to be sure, but rules nevertheless. Some realists, however, think it is a mistake to think of laws as rules. They believe that the objections Gray raises to thinking of organs other than courts as makers of rules of law can be pushed further in order to show that there are no rules at all. One might wonder *why* it matters whether we do or do not think in terms of rules, so long as the central role of judges and courts is acknowledged. Perhaps the thought is that if rules are brought in at any point, they may have a carry-over effect from decision to decision—that is, they may impose limits on judges, limits that have no official standing, and that should not be allowed to constrain the judicial mind in arriving at its decisions. Jerome Frank interprets Gray as saying that though all law is made by judges, not all judicial decisions are acts of law-making. Only in some decisions do judges promulgate rules of law; in other decisions they follow rules that they or other judges have promulgated in prior decisions. Frank says that, according to Gray there is such a thing as "the law of Massachusetts," such that if a judge decides a case contrary to that law without promulgating a new rule, he is in error.[32] Frank remarks that "for all his terse directness, you will detect more than a trace of the old philosophy in Gray's views. You will note his constant reiteration of the words 'rules' and 'principles.' Gray defines law not as what the courts decide but as the '*rules* which the courts lay down for the determination of legal rights and duties' or 'the *rules of decision* which the courts lay down.' "[33]

The position of Frank and other realists is that there are no rules at all in the sense in which Gray thinks of them. There are no rules because, if there were, things would be nailed down, legally speaking, in a way that they are not, and judges would be bound to give certain results in a way that they are not. How, realists ask, can there be a rule that judges are *bound* to follow if judges can carve exceptions out of rules, or if, since rules are not self-applying, a creative act by a judge is required in order for a result to be reached? Again, how can we think in terms of rules that dictate judicial decisions if judicial discretion is as broad as it is; if different judges can, through sound uses of their discretion, reach different results; and if, consequently, there is no uniquely correct result to be reached? And, finally, how can the picture of law as a set of rules be viewed as anything but a myth when juries are as free as they in fact are (via the device of the general verdict) to ignore (if indeed they understand) the court's instructions on the applicable law?[34]

A more metaphysical objection to the idea of the existence of rules of law is that rules are not real things; they do not exist as distinct entities in the world. They exist only in the mind.[35] Being mental existents, they are made by human beings, and like anything else made by human beings they are made for certain human purposes—namely, to organize past experience in a way that will make it a useful tool. Rules, so understood, are useful in learning about the law and in trying to predict the future course of the law. But such rules cannot require that a judge reach one decision rather than another, any more than the fact that a person usually behaves in a certain way in certain circumstances requires him to behave that way in the future.

THE NATURE OF LAW

In their writings realists do not present systematic accounts of the nature of law; indeed, such an enterprise is largely foreign to their aims. Nevertheless, some ideas about the nature of law can be gleaned from their writings. One realist view of the nature of the law is found in the writings of Oliver Wendell Holmes. In some ways Holmes's view of law is, on some interpretations, similar to Gray's. In a key sentence Holmes says, "The prophesies of what the courts will do in fact, and nothing more pretentious, are what I mean by the law."[36] Interpreted in the light of the following passage this might suggest a Gray-like picture of law: "The life of the law has not been logic: it has been experience. The felt necessities of the time, the prevalent moral and political theories, intuitions of public policy . . . have had a good deal more to do than the syllogism in determining the rules by which men should be governed. The law embodies the story of a nation's development through many centuries."[37] Citing these statements, Edgar Bodenheimer says of Holmes that he "regarded law largely as a body of edicts representing the will of the dominant interests in society, backed by force."[38]

The sentence in question is usually given a different interpretation, however. On this interpretation Holmes means that to say something is the law is merely to say something about what a court is likely to decide if a given case comes before it. This view of law reflects a certain concern that Holmes and other realists share—namely, a concern with achieving some sort of control over things by being able to predict what is going to happen. Lawyers, for example, need to advise their clients, and the citizenry at large needs to know how to handle its affairs. In order to do these things one needs, not knowledge of some abstract rules and principles of law, but the ability to predict what judges will decide if and when a given case comes up. We will always be in the best position to say what the law is, according to Holmes, if we take the point of view of the bad man—that is, the point of view of the person who wants to know not some abstract principle or verbal rule, but what is likely to happen to him if he does one thing rather than another.[39] Hence the view that law is a prediction of what courts will do.

Though Holmes's advice may well be salutary for some purposes, critics have pointed out that it will not do as an analysis of the nature of law (yet, in fairness, it should be said that the writings in which Holmes expressed some of these views were probably not intended as philosophical disquisitions on the nature of law). For one thing, the view that so-called rules of law are merely predictions of judicial behavior "can at best apply to statements of law ventured by private individuals or their advisers. It cannot apply to the courts' own statements of a legal rule."[40] The reason for this is that a court, in saying that something *is* the law, is not predicting how it is going to decide the case: an observer may predict what a judge is going to do, but a judge cannot, in deciding a case, merely be predicting what he is going to do; he is doing it. Second, though the point of view of the bad man is appropriate for some purposes, there are other points of view from which to regard the law. There is the point of view of the good man, the man who sincerely wants to know what is expected of him so that he can conform his behavior to these legal expectations. Certainly there are such persons, and it may even be that this is the attitude of most people most of the time. Why, then, should not a characterization of law take this as its point of view?*

Perhaps the most extreme realist view of law is that expressed by such writers as Jerome Frank, Karl Llewellyn, and Richard Taylor, at least as set forth in their best-known writings on the subject. Law, according to Frank, consists of the sum total of all individual decisions:

We may now venture a rough definition of law from the point of view of the average man: For any particular lay person, the law, with respect to any particular set of facts, is a decision of a court with respect to those facts so far as that decision affects that particular person. Until a court has passed on those facts no law on that subject is yet in existence. Prior to such a decision, the only law available is the opinion of lawyers as to the law relating to that person and to those facts. Such opinion is not actually law but only a guess as to what a court will decide.

Law, then, as to any given situation is either (a) actual law, i.e., a specific past decision, as to that situation, or (b) probable law, i.e., a guess as to a specific future decision.[41]

As Frank sees it, the law can differ from case to case, however similar those cases may be. That is, there is no such thing, strictly speaking, as *the* law on a given subject; there is the law of this particular case, the law of that particular case, and so on, for however many cases there are. Frank's thought here seems to be that

---

* We will see later, in Chapter 4, that H. L. A. Hart develops an impressive view of the nature of law based on this point of view.

there is no point in asserting that the law on a given subject is contrary to a court's decision in a particular case, for such a claim would make no difference to any of the litigants. "Whichever court gives the decision, that decision is all the law there is, in any practical sense, for the parties to the suit."[42] What is relevant for our understanding of law is what actually happens in the courts—*all* the courts—and if different courts give different decisions in similar cases, then there is more than one law involved.

This view is defended by Richard Taylor:

[T]he law in any particular case is not the written enactment, in case such exists, and not the common law, and certainly not some unwritten natural law, but precisely the judicial decision itself.... No actual meaning can be given to the idea of an *illegal* judicial decision. . . . The law for a litigant is the statement of his legal obligation. And that statement is nothing other than a judicial decision. His obligation under the law comes into existence with the rendering of that decision, in no way exists until then, and is, from then on, abolished, if at all, only by another judicial decision.[43]

The law is to be found in judicial decisions, and the *only* law there is is embodied in the judge's decision. It makes no difference if a judicial decision is at odds with precedent or with statutes or whatever; the law *to the parties* is what the judge decides, unless some higher court decides differently, in which case *that* decision is the law to the parties. As an example, Taylor offers, among others, the case of *Riggs* v. *Palmer*.[44] In this case the defendant, Elmer Palmer, was named as a legatee in his grandfather's will. Fearing the will would be changed, defendant murdered his grandfather, for which he was sent to jail. The other legatees sued to prevent defendant from acquiring the property left to him in the will. The court acknowledged that under the relevant statutes defendant was entitled to the property, but it nevertheless held that he could not inherit under the will. Taylor comments:

Now we are not here concerned with whether the court decided wisely or foolishly. . . . The questions to be asked are rather these: "What were Elmer Palmer's legal rights with respect to the property after the appellate decision?" "Did the [other legatees] then have ownership of the farm?" Both of these questions turn entirely on this one: "What was the law for the litigants?" The answer to this is not subject to controversy. The law was not what any statute declared it to be, for the law here was one thing and the statute the opposite. The law was not any clear principle derived from the common law. The law was found entirely in the opinion of the majority of the court, and *consisted* entirely of that opinion.[45]

It is "the actual decisions of courts that litigants must live with,"[46] and it is thus the sum of all these individual decisions that constitutes the law. The law is everything that is finally enforced by the legal system. We have here the culmination of realist attacks on the conception of the law of a society being a set of rules: there are no rules of law at all, but rather as many laws as there are judicial decisions.

THE ROLE OF JUDGES

What, according to realists, should judges do in deciding cases, if their task is not to find and apply the law or even to make rules of law? What judges should *not* do, realists maintain, is involve themselves with problems about what words mean. It is futile, they say, to try to answer questions such as whether something is or is not a corporation, or whether it is domiciled in a given state. This point is made very nicely by Felix S. Cohen:

The Supreme Court argued, "A labor union can be sued because it is, in essential aspects, a person, a quasi-corporation." The realist will say, "A labor union is a person or quasi-corporation because it can be sued; to call something a person in law, is merely to state, in metaphorical language, that it can be sued."

There is a significant difference between these two ways of describing the situation. If we say that a court acts in a certain way "because a labor union is a person," we *appear to justify the court's action,* and to justify that action, moreover, in transcendental terms, by asserting something that sounds like a proposition but which *can not be confirmed or refuted by positive evidence or by ethical argument.* If, on the other hand, we say that a labor union is a person "because the courts allow it to be sued," we recognize that the action of the courts has not been justified at all, and that the question of whether the action of the courts is justifiable calls for an answer in non-legal terms. To justify or criticize legal rules in purely legal terms is always to argue in a vicious circle.[47]

In short, there are appropriate and inappropriate types of justifications for judicial decisions, and the appropriate types are the
ones that squarely face the issues by recognizing that moral choices
are being made, rather than hiding these choices behind verbal
or "paper" rules.

Most realists do not content themselves with pointing this out,
however; they usually have ideas about how the issues are squarely
to be faced and dealt with. Judges should try to get clear about
the effects of deciding one way or another, and then reach their
decisions in accordance with an evaluation of these effects:

> If deduction does not solve cases, but only shows the effect of a given
> premise; and if there is available a competing but equally authoritative
> premise that leads to a different conclusion—then there is a choice in
> the case; a choice to be justified; a choice which *can* be justified only
> as a question of policy. . . . [O]nly policy considerations and the facing
> of policy considerations can justify "interpreting" . . . the relevant body
> of precedent in one way or in another.[48]

In evaluating these effects and in selecting policies, some writers
recommend that the aim should be to balance the competing interests involved in a case;[49] and most writers make the closely related
recommendation that judges should aim to promote social welfare.
It is often urged that many legal problems might profitably be
decided in terms of the appropriate allocation of risks in society,
and indeed a good deal of judicial activity in tort and business
matters has come to reflect this approach.

THE TASK OF JURISPRUDENCE

Realists, as we have noted, play down abstract questions about
the nature of law. Their jurisprudential interests are more practically oriented, exhibiting a primary concern for the functioning
of the judicial process, which they wish to explain and improve.
Thus, one aim of jurisprudence, as realists see it, is to study the
judicial process in order to see how decisions are actually made,
with an eye to increasing the predictability of judicial decisions.
As George Christie notes, "[realists] have reminded us that, whatever the shortcomings of the theories put forward by the realists

themselves, no theory of legal reasoning and of the legal process is worth serious consideration if it does not in fact permit us to predict the outcome of judicial decisions."[50] And Jerome Frank tells us that "the way in which the judge gets his hunches is the key to the judicial process. Whatever produces the judge's hunches makes the law."[51] Thus, jurisprudence must learn something about what motivates judges, both collectively and individually; in particular, the background and character of judges and the impact of these on judicial behavior must be brought to light. Even what judges eat for breakfast is relevant, since it can affect decisions. (This kind of jurisprudence has sometimes been referred to, unflatteringly, as gastronomic jurisprudence.) What is not completely clear is why this sort of predictability of the judicial decision is a desirable thing for jurisprudence to pursue. We might perhaps view it as a throwback to the aims of "old-fashioned" jurisprudence, which sought certainty in the legal process (according to Frank) by inventing a mythical uniformity and regularity in the law. On the other hand, realists think of jurisprudence as a branch of the social sciences, and just as the aims of science in general are the aims of such disciplines as psychology and sociology, perhaps they are also appropriate aims of legal "science."

Another aim of jurisprudence, according to realists, is the study of judges' opinions in order to find the "real" or motivating reasons behind the decisions that are made. Karl Llewellyn remarks that "study has been attempted of 'substantive rules' in the particular light of the available remedial procedure; the hope being to discover in the court's unmentioned knowledge of the immediate consequences of this rule or that, in the case at hand, a motivation which cuts deeper than any shown by the opinion."[52] And he refers mysteriously to "hidden factors" that if brought to light might make predictions more certain. Related to the search for the "real" reason for a judicial decision is a desire to look through words to realities, to see what is really going on when one decision rather than another is made—that is, to see what the impact of each of the possibilities would be. Rules are at best words on paper; but paper rules, when applied, promote or protect certain interests at the expense of others. Judges who push around paper rules may or may not advert to these effects; but in any event efforts should be made to bring these matters to light.

One thing that such a concentration on the effects of judicial decisions requires of jurisprudence, as most realists see it, is detailed sociological or other study. Such empirical work is thought to be necessary so that the proper policy considerations can be brought to bear on judicial decisions. (There is an important and difficult problem here for the judicial process, namely, how such information, or any factual information not part of the evidence of a given case, is to come to the attention of judges. Sometimes it comes in by way of the doctrine of judicial notice; but for the most part it is a matter of a process of slow infiltration into the legal conscious-ness—or subconscious. In *Brown* v. *Board of Education of Topeka,* for example, the Supreme Court cited some psychological litera-ture in support of its claim that segregation has adverse effects on people.[53])

Though empirical studies are thought to be important matters for jurisprudence, equally important, if not more so, is work on the ends that the law is to promote. One of the most prominent ideas here is that the legal processes are concerned with conflicts of interest, and that the judicial process is (whether officials know it or not), and should be, concerned with identifying and balanc-ing these interests. This is the view, for example, of Roscoe Pound, who has had a tremendous impact on American jurisprudence:

A legal system attains the end of the legal order, or at any rate strives to do so, by recognizing certain . . . interests, by defining the limits with-in which those interests shall be recognized and given effect through legal precepts developed and applied by the judicial (and today the administrative) process according to an authoritative technique, and by endeavoring to secure the interests so recognized within defined limits.

. . . .

If we look at the actual working out, development, and application of legal precepts rather than at juristic theory, we may say that three methods have obtained. One is a finding out by experience of what will achieve an adjustment of conflicting and overlapping interests with the least impairment of the scheme of interests as a whole and giving that experience a reasoned development.[54]

In many of his articles—in particular, "A Survey of Social Interests" and "A Survey of Public Interests"—Pound has sought to bring to light the various interests that are at stake in judicial decision making, and that should be protected or advanced by the courts.[55] He asks, "Why should not the lawyer make a survey of legal systems in order to ascertain just what [interests] have pressed or are now pressing for recognition and satisfaction and how far they have been or are now recognized and secured?" He then makes this very illuminating comment: "This is precisely what has been done in the case of individual interests, in the scheme of natural rights, although the process has usually been covered up by a pretentious fabric of logical deduction. The same method may well be applied to social interests, and this should be done consciously and avowedly, as befits the science of today."[56]

TWO PROBLEMS FOR REALISM

Some of the realists' ideas about law seem to lead to difficulties having to do with the character and role of legal institutions within the political framework. These problems will be raised as part of the exposition of legal realism, but will not be discussed at any length here. The first problem concerns the view of some realists, most notably Pound in the United States, that the law and the judicial process are concerned with the balancing of interests. Judges are faced with clashes of interests, and their task is to resolve these conflicts. The inference seems sometimes to be drawn that in this task courts are no different from any other institution that resolves conflicts of interest. The judicial process may thus come to be looked on as one among many political institutions in a society, faced with the same tasks as those institutions and dealing with them in substantially the same way (e.g. making compromises and the like), though perhaps with a bit of ceremony that makes it look as if something else is going on. How, one might ask, can it be otherwise where there are competing interests—that is, according to Pound, competing claims, demands, or desires. This conception of the roles of courts and judges is certainly not a flattering one. It is at odds with our usual conception of our judicial institutions, which for the most part we see as quite different from straightforwardly political institutions.

An answer to this must first of all explain the difference between interests, on the one hand, and claims, demands, and desires on the other, and then it must make a distinction between the balancing of interests and compromise. And then, these distinctions having been drawn, something must be done to meet Llewellyn's challenge that Pound's insights have not been fruitful because the " 'balancing of interests' remains with no indication of how to tell an interest when you see one, much less with any study of how they are or should be balanced."[57] These problems are, I believe, resolvable, but will not be pursued here.[58]

The second problem for the realists concerns the role of the judiciary in a democracy. Realists tell us that judges legislate, and some realists even insist there is no law that does not originate in the judiciary. Most realists have applauded this fact, for it provides great opportunity for reform efforts. Indeed, realists were in the vanguard of reform for a good many years, and their intellectual heirs—some contemporary legal sociologists—still have a reforming impact on the law.* But legislative activity by judges seems to be at odds with the theory of democracy. For in judges we have persons who, though not elected (or if elected, usually not seriously subject to removal by the electorate) and not even supposed to be responsive to public opinion, are nevertheless in a position to make law—a task that in a democracy is thought to be the prerogative of elected representatives. Some of this judicial legislation, to be sure, consists of no more than the interpretation of vague language, and might be considered both unavoidable and negligible; but many realists assure us that it goes further than this, arguing that judges are in a position to bring about any results they want—and presumably sometimes do so (some realists being or having been judges). This is, of course, a worrisome problem,

---

* The legal sociologists will be discussed later, in Chapter 3.

and some who see no way out of it have suggested, apparently seriously and perhaps cynically, that "judges will serve the public interest better if they keep quiet about their legislative function. No doubt they will discreetly contribute to changes in the law, because they cannot do otherwise, even if they would. But the judge who shows his hand, who advertises what he is about [is] doing more harm to general confidence in the law as a constant, safe in the hands of the judges, than he is doing to the law's credit as a set of rules nicely attuned to the sentiment of the day."[59]

Problems concerning the role of the judiciary in a democracy can probably be given a satisfactory resolution. The issues involved are much the same as those that come up in connection with the issue of judicial review, which has seemed to some to be incompatible with democracy, and for the same reasons. Of course, it is one thing to resolve the problem from the standpoint of political theory—that is, to produce a democratic political theory in which a certain degree of legislatively oriented judicial activity is justifiable. It is quite another thing to determine the precise allowable degree of that activity.

But neither of these matters will be pursued here. In the next chapter a critique of the realist argument against the notion of legal rules will be undertaken.

2

Legal Realism and Rules of Law

It is probably correct to say that realism is the prevailing legal philosophy among teachers and practitioners of law in the United States, and among many legal scholars. This view of law and the legal process is associated with such important jurists and scholars as Oliver Wendell Holmes, Joseph Bingham, Jerome Frank, Eugen Ehrlich, and Karl Llewellyn. The emphasis of this philosophy, as the name suggests, has been an insistence on being realistic about the law and its processes. This emphasis is evident in Holmes's famous remark that "the life of the law has not been logic: it has been experience," a pronouncement that has often been taken as the hallmark of realism.[1]

The aspect of realism we are primarily concerned with here is its rejection of the idea that there are rules of law—rules, that is, that have weight in the law, that have authority, for realists are usually willing to accept as rules (or better "rules") the statements of law that are written down in law books, and that teachers teach and students learn, so long as these statements ("rules") are not thought of as having any authority. Such statements are merely shorthand reports of what is usually decided in courts, and thus predictions of what can be expected to be decided in future cases; they are useful, they have instrumental value.

In the following discussion, then, what we want to examine is the realist's skepticism toward the idea that there are rules in law with authority, and in particular the realist's arguments for this position. But before we begin, let me point out that the arguments to be considered are not the arguments of any particular legal realist; no realist (to my knowledge) has maintained each and every one of them, but all have been advanced by some realist or other. So, though I use expressions like "the realist says" or "the realist position is," these are to be understood as merely representative.

REALISM AS A REACTION

In one light the realist position can be seen as a reaction to certain metaphysical views about law. In what might roughly be called Platonically inspired theories of law, rules and principles have an other-worldly existence; they exist in that world whether or not actually thought of by human beings, though humans can come to grasp them. Now such a view has the virtue of explaining what is taken to be an important datum—the bindingness of law. That is, it explains the supposed fact that law is binding quite irrespective of the prospect of sanctions for noncompliance and quite irrespective of calculations of self-interest. Law, in this view, is binding in much the same way that any fact is binding. One is constrained to make the appropriate responses to the truths of the universe, whether this is a matter of believing the laws describing the operation of the universe or of acting in accordance with the laws prescribing how we are to behave. In either case it is the indisputable fact, the truth, that has a hold on us, and that in the case of prescriptive facts or truths accounts for the bindingness of law. But even if such a metaphysical position were to explain the bindingness of law (a question that will not be taken up here), such a view naturally suggests the theory of the judicial process that realists reject. This is the theory, advanced most influentially by Blackstone, though not in these words, that the law is "out there"; that judicial decision-making is simply a matter of discovering the appropriate legal rule, and of applying this rule to the facts of a case so as to deduce the correct result; that judges do not "make" law, i.e. legislate; and that when a judge overrules a precedent he is merely announcing that the rule stated or otherwise embodied in the prior case was not a rule of law at all, that the prior case was mistaken, and that the rule now formulated is (and was) the correct one, the one that was "there" all along but not correctly apprehended. This view of the judicial process, realists point out, does not square with the facts, the reality, as revealed to us in everyday experience. Law is not, in Holmes's ringing phrase a "brooding omnipresence in the sky."[2] Arriving at a judicial decision is not a matter of finding and applying a ready-made rule; judges *do* legislate; judicial decision-making is a creative, not a mechanical, activity.

There are other metaphysical positions that realists equally oppose, and for the same reasons. As some see it, the problem is this: "Law is conceived at the same time as an observable phenomenon in the world of facts, and as a binding norm in the world of morals and rules, at the same time as physical and metaphysical, as empirical and *a priori,* as real and ideal, as something that exists and something that is valid."[3] What might be called the Kantian type of response to this apparent dualism is to distinguish between the empirical self, which is the self we confront in everyday experience and which laws of psychology are about, and a nonempirical or transcendental self, which is a necessary presupposition of our moral (and legal) thinking. Law is tied up with the metaphysical self, for without this presupposition we cannot account for the categorical and absolute bindingness of legal norms —that is, without the presupposition we cannot account for categorical obligation of any sort, including that found in the legal order.[4] But such views leave us with the problem of how to connect the law, so understood, with actual legislative and judicial processes, and it is these, the realist insists, that are the objects of our common concern and our study. The notion of a valid rule of law embedded in these theories is seen to be the culprit, for it is thought to lead to the theory of the judicial process mentioned above, which is the main target of the realist's animadversions.

We are bound to note, however, that the notion of valid rules of law plays a role in other legal philosophies that are not so metaphysically oriented, and thus a defense of this notion is not necessarily a defense of the metaphysics that has sparked many of the realists' criticisms. The realists do not perhaps argue in so many words that there are no binding rules because (or just because) these metaphysical positions are mistaken. Nevertheless, some of their arguments seem to have force only in the context of these metaphysical views.

THE REALIST ARGUMENTS AGAINST LEGAL RULES AND SOME RESPONSES

As we have seen, the idea that there are rules of law is often taken to be responsible for the notion that there is a phenomenon of bindingness in law, and so realists have attacked the idea that there are rules of law—that there is in a legal system a "body of law" made up of a set of authoritative rules, and that the "rule of law" is just the authority of these rules. In an attempt to bring some order to the discussion of these arguments, I have classified them into two groups: those relying on facts about and problems inherent in the machinery of law, and those bringing out problems inherent in the nature of rules or in the nature of the law, or both. Some of these arguments shade into one another, so that what is said about one might well apply also to others. These arguments all have the same general structure, as follows. The existence of rules implies that certain things are true of a legal system, that certain phenomena must be present in the legal universe. But things are not in fact this way; things are much looser or less nailed down than would have to be the case if rules existed. Therefore, there are no rules in a legal system.

Arguments Based on the Machinery of Law

1. Judges, says the realist, do not, in deciding cases, thumb through the sources of law, hunting for a rule that they then apply to the facts to reach a decision—as if they had no idea what result

they were going to reach before they found the appropriate rule. The judicial judgment is, instead, often intuitive, and reasons for a decision are often tacked on after it has been made.

Now these may be correct observations about how judicial decisions are made. But they do not show there are no rules in law, for the explanation of this phenomenon may simply be that the judge knows the law so well that he (or she) knows or reaches the correct result without consciously applying a rule. A rule theorist can acknowledge the judicial hunch, and will insist only that the reasons given in support of the decision be strong enough to *justify* the result. That is, he will insist that the result actually reached be the result that should have been reached, and that would have been reached if there had been, prior to the decision, a deliberate advertence to the rules. Of course, a judge may be dishonest; he might reach a decision that he knows to be improper, and then rationalize it (in the pejorative sense of that term), i.e. make it look good. Undoubtedly this sometimes occurs, and it needs to be mentioned in any description of legal institutions. There are even theoretical difficulties presented by such cases (when they become known, of course), concerning whether they ought to have weight as precedent. But such occurrences do not by themselves show there are no rules of law; they show only that judges may sometimes fail—deliberately—to act in accordance with them.

2. Judges have power, the realist points out. A judge can usually decide a case in any way he wants. There may be power elsewhere in the legal system or in the larger political system to change a judicial decision or mitigate its effects; but there is much effective power in the judiciary. Accordingly, it cannot be said that a judge is *bound* to decide a case one way rather than another; hence a legal system does not consist of rules that bind a judge.

Here again, we may acknowledge the correctness of the observation that judges have power of this sort. But it does not follow from this that a judge cannot be bound. There is a distinction between being bound in the sense of being threatened or coerced or pressured into doing something, and being bound in the sense of having a requirement imposed on one; and it is possible to be bound in the latter sense without being bound in the former sense. Where such power exists, of course, the possibility of abuse exists, too. But the problem, then, is how to limit that power in ways that will prevent its abuses but not its legitimate uses; the mere existence of the power to abuse does not by itself indicate any difficulties for the existence of rules.

3. Even where judicial power is not abused, though, different courts and different judges can and do reach different results in similar and even in the same cases. Since this is so, says the realist, there can be no sense in which a judge is bound to reach one result rather than another, and from this it follows that there are no rules, if rules are thought of as binding.

There is a simple reply to this argument, namely: just because two judges, without abusing their authority, give different results, it does not follow that neither of them is mistaken; it is only that at least one of them has not reached the best possible result. This reply will probably seem unsatisfactory to some, notably those who argue that because different judges reach different results one judgment cannot sensibly be said to be better than another, and so the final result is determined not by which decision is more nearly right, but by what the higher court says. But this is a different objection, and will be considered later.

4. Karl Llewellyn, in "A Realistic Jurisprudence—the Next Step" and elsewhere, inveighs against what he calls "paper rules" and the magic of words. Part of what he is attacking, I take it, is the insistence that some verbal formulation of a rule, written down somewhere, is the law. We must distinguish, he tells us, between law in books and law in practice; and it is a mistake to call paper rules the law if they are not what people act in accordance with and may not even be what judges enforce.[5]

This argument, like the previous one, seems to be masking a different objection, for the simple answer is that it may be either that the formulation of a rule is mistaken or that people (and even judges) are ignoring the law. The latter possibility suggests that what was once the law may have somehow, without explicit repeal or overruling, ceased to be the law (due, for example, to desuetude), and even that a new law may have somehow been substituted for an old one; but this does not mean there are no rules of law.

5. The objection Llewellyn probably means to raise is this one, which has been raised by Joseph Bingham. Rules are supposed to impose binding requirements on us, and particularly on judges. But what kinds of things are rules? Where do they exist? "Principles and rules cannot exist outside the mind. . . . They are . . . not external things discovered and abstracted by the mind."[6] As (mere) mental existents, rules can serve only the functions of organizing data and helping us to make predictions of what courts will do; they are tools, and are valid only so long as they lead to successful predictions. Thus rules have no authority with us—that is, there are no rules in the sense with which we are here concerned.

This argument, however, is defective as it stands, for it requires the premise that only an extra-mentally existing rule can have authority with us (or, alternatively, that no mentally existing rule —if rules of law are properly construed as mental existents—can have authority with us). This is, of course, a very important premise, for one of the critical questions in any area of behavior governance is whether *anything* can have authority with us, and if so how. But Bingham merely assumes, without argument, that no mental existent could have such authority.

Bingham suggests a second difficulty with accepting the existence of rules, however—namely, the problem of how there can be a rule of law if there is no clear, unambiguous, and authoritative statement of what it is. This is connected with the metaphysical problem mentioned earlier, the idea being that if rules exist in some other-worldly realm, then they can be conceived of as clear and authoritative. But, the argument goes, when we look around this world, trying to find what the supposed rules of law are, we find only different people having different ideas about what the rules are. Hence, there are no legal rules.

The reply to this argument is the same as the reply to the third one, and will seem unsatisfactory to many for the same reason: none of this shows there is no proper statement of the rule. Later, we shall consider the claim that there cannot be a proper statement of the rule.

6. Judicial decision-making is a creative activity, the realist argues. Judges do not merely discover what the law is, they take a hand in making it. If this is so, then the law cannot be thought of in terms of rules, and to think of it in this way is to think in mythical terms about judicial decision-making and fail to see what the real bases of judicial decisions are.

Now the teaching and writings of legal realists have certainly been salutary in bringing people to see what is often going on in judicial decision-making; in particular, that it is often not a matter of discovering what is antecedently the case. But to say that the law coming out of a decision sometimes does not exist prior to that decision is *not* to say that there are no rules of law. For it is compatible with the facts about how the judicial process works that what the judge is doing is making a new rule. Believing in rules of law does not require us to say that all rules must exist prior to decision. And rule-theorists need not be committed to what is called mechanical jurisprudence (which in its most problematic aspect has to do not with syllogistic reasoning, but with the major premises of such pieces of reasoning).

7. Still another realist argument centers on the fact that the decisions of courts—at least those of the highest court in a legal system—are final.[7] Thus, within a legal system the claim that the decision of the highest court is mistaken, that the rule of law in a particular case is something other than the court has held, is without significance because without legal effect. Hence, there is no point in speaking of rules of law, if this implies that the courts could be mistaken, or at least if it implies that there is any importance in saying a court is mistaken.

H. L. A. Hart has answered an argument of this sort along these lines: the fact that a judge has the last word does not imply there is no rule, any more than the fact that the scorer in a game might make a mistake implies there is no scoring rule.[8] Further, the claim that there is no point in speaking of rules of law due to the finality of judicial decisions seems wrong. Even judges can learn from mistakes, so there is always reason to point out that a mistake has been made, and why.*

Arguments Based on the Nature of Rules or of Law

8. As has often been pointed out, the law is not self-applying.[9] That is, a law cannot, by itself, indicate exactly which sets of factual circumstances are covered by it and which are not; by necessity a law must be general, must apply to more than one case. Further, a law must be expressed in words, and words are "open-textured": "uncertainty at the borderline is the price to be paid for the use of general classifying terms in any form of communication concerning matters of fact."[10] Now given that all of this is true, as it seems to be, what conclusion is to be drawn? It might be concluded that these facts show that the law does not consist of rules, because rules would not have these features. Rules would nail things down in such a way that there could be no doubt about what citizens and judges are to do.

The short answer, to begin with, is that if we accept this argument, we must then agree that there are virtually no rules in any area of human activity. For no rules, or at any rate very few rules, can be self-applying in the sense that there can be no doubt whether certain cases fall within them or not, and this is because all rules, being expressed in words that are open-textured, are vague. All rules have what Hart calls penumbral areas.[11] So if this argument is sound, it applies to all so-called rules, of games as well

* In addition, Ronald Dworkin argues ("A Theory of Civil Disobedience," in Howard E. Kiefer and Milton K. Munitz, eds., *Ethics and Social Justice*, Albany, N.Y., 1968, p. 232) that the distinction between what the law is and "any particular person's view of what the law is" is important in the justification of civil disobedience, and he cites Holmes's drawing of this disinction in his dissent in Gitlow v. New York, 268 U.S. 652, 45 S. Ct. 625, 69 L. Ed. 1138 (1925). In making this distinction Dworkin explicitly disclaims its dependence on any of the metaphysical views mentioned earlier. Contrast George C. Christie, "Objectivity in the Law," *Yale Law Journal,* 78 (1969): 1322n.

as law. Since there are certainly rules of games, this argument does not show there are no rules of law.

But why, in any event, should it be the case that rules could exist only if self-applying? Perhaps because the circumstance of open texture is thought to support a different argument against the existence of rules of law. Since rules are not self-applying, some official must decide whether a rule is to apply in a particular case, and making such judgments involves an exercise of discretion. The very necessity of discretion in a legal system, says the realist, shows that a legal system cannot be thought of as involving rules. Our question, then, is, what is it about the existence of discretion that leads him to that conclusion? One answer might be that having discretion implies having power, and one who has power cannot be bound. But it is false that one who has power cannot be, in the appropriate sense, bound; this was discussed in connection with the second argument, above. The existence of discretion does, however, present difficulties, as we shall shortly see.

9. So-called rules of law have exceptions. Some of these exceptions are not problematic: where an exception is explicitly built into the law, it is not an exception to the law itself, but part of the law. For example, a law setting maximum speed limits might make exceptions for ambulances, fire trucks, and other vehicles. These exceptions pose problems only if one thinks that rules must be very simple, applying, for example, to all vehicles as a class with no provision for any subclass.

More problematic are the cases where there is no explicit, built-in exception, but where a judge makes an exception to an apparently exceptionless rule. For example, a judge might make an exception to the speed limit for private citizens rushing people to hospitals, perhaps on the ground that the aim of the laws that limit speed is furthered, not hindered, by permitting such an exception. This is not a case of vagueness, for the law as it exists (in the example) is quite clear; the case in question thus belongs to what Hart calls the "core of certainty."[12] It is important to be clear about this. There is a difference between deciding what cases a vague law is applicable to and making an exception to a law, for there can be exceptions only when the law to which an exception is being made would otherwise apply. And though those who are charged with applying the law must, logically, have discretion to decide whether terms are vague and to fix the range of application of vague terms, they need not, logically, have discretion to make exceptions in cases where there is no vagueness.

The making of exceptions by judges poses a difficulty for the notion of rules of law only if one thinks that a rule theory requires that rules exist prior to judicial decision. But there is no need to hold such a view; a rule theory can acknowledge that sometimes judges make new rules, or at least change old ones.[13] For example, the court in *Riggs* v. *Palmer* (see Chapter 1, p. 14) can be taken to have changed the applicable rule from, roughly, "All those named as legatees in wills may inherit" to "All those named as legatees in wills who have not criminally brought about the death of the testator may inherit."

10. There is more discretion in a legal system (at least there is in our legal system) than is required by the need to apply vague rules. Sometimes there are explicit grants of discretionary authority —where a law, for example, says merely that judges shall, in the exercise of their sound discretion, grant continuances on the application of the parties in a case. And a third area of discretionary authority has to do with the making of exceptions to rules, where the exceptions are not built into the rules themselves. (In referring to discretionary authority and not discretionary power, I am supposing that we are concerned with legitimate, not abusive, exercises of discretion; the power to abuse discretion was discussed in points 1 and 2, above.)

The first of these three areas of discretion—the applying of vague rules—involves what Ronald Dworkin calls a weak sense of discretion, in which an official must use his judgment because the rule in question "cannot be applied mechanically." The second area of discretion involves what Dworkin calls a strong sense of discretion, for no standards have been given to the judge in our example of the granting of continuances; the judge must both determine what standards to apply and then apply them. The third area of discretion is both like and unlike Dworkin's strong sense. It is like the strong sense in that the judge has no standards telling him how, and even when, to make exceptions to rules. Indeed, there is usually (and perhaps always) no explicit grant of authority to do this, and it is in this respect that the third area of discretion is unlike the strong sense. As Dworkin sees it, this would not count as discretion at all, for "the concept of discretion is at home only in one sort of context: when someone is in general charged with making decisions subject to standards set by a particular authority. . . . Discretion, like the hole in a doughnut, does not exist except as an area left open by a surrounding belt of restriction."[14] But though on the one hand there are usually no "standards set by a particular authority" when it comes to writing exceptions into rules (or, more noticeably, when it comes to rewriting pieces of the common law), on the other hand it would be a mistake to say there are no restrictions on what judges are permitted to do; there are at least certain principles in a legal system, to which Dworkin has drawn our attention, that serve as restrictions.* Thus I think we may reasonably call this third area of judicial activity discretionary.

What problem does the existence of all this discretion pose for the view that there are rules of law? The realist says that since there is discretion, there is no uniquely correct result. It is not merely that different judges reach different results, and so at least one of them must be regarded as being mistaken; it is rather that there *is* no correct result, so that neither of them can properly be said to be mistaken. If there were rules, the realist argues, this would not be so: there *could* be a uniquely correct result. Hence, there are no rules.

Now realists do not, to my knowledge, indicate why the concept of a rule should be incompatible with the indeterminacy of the results that are actually reached. Part of it seems to be the idea that rules are supposed to *bind,* and that this is impossible if there is looseness in what the result in a case will actually be. However, the rules that some legal theorists argue for are, by their very nature, general; if they were not, they could not do the jobs

* Legal principles will be discussed in Chapters 4 and 5.

for which we require them.[15] So one would think that realists could happily acknowledge the existence of rules of this sort, and still go on to make all of their points about vagueness and discretion. Instead, they seem to have a conception of rules according to which the existence of a rule nails everything down, never leaving any doubt about how people should behave and about what results judges should reach.[16] Obviously, if this is what rules are, there are few or no rules of law. But this view seems to confuse particular instructions ("Do this now") with general instructions ("When in circumstances c, do x"); rules are more like the latter than the former, and so is the law.

Be that as it may, there is still the question of whether there can be uniquely correct results in judicial decision-making. For, as I have said, this is what seems to be the realist's real target, whether or not he is correct in thinking that the possibility of uniquely correct results and the concept of rules are logically connected. The argument might be: rules are thought of as things that bind; in order to bind they must yield uniquely correct results; they do not yield such results; so, there are no rules. This argument will be discussed at some length in the next section.

11. Within constitutional limitations on the scope of legislative authority, legislatures may pass any laws at all; more important, legislatures in different jurisdictions can pass different laws on the same subject, and there is no uniquely correct legislative response to a problem. Similarly, the realist might argue, judges make law, and this implies that there should be nothing untoward about their reaching different results in similar cases—in other words, there is no uniquely correct result. Discussion of the main point of this argument will be put off until later. But three comments can be made at this stage. First, judicial legislation, despite the characterization, is not necessarily the same as the full-blooded case of legislation. Judicial legislation appears to be subject to more restrictions; for example, courts are bound by their institutional character in a way that legislatures are not bound. Second, it is not as obvious as this analogy suggests that there can be no uniquely correct result even with regard to the standard kind of

legislation. This leads to the third comment, which is that the notion of a uniquely correct result has not been made clear. The claim that there cannot be a uniquely correct result must be distinguished from the claim that there can be such a result, though we may not be certain, and may disagree, about what it is.

12. A last but very important realist argument is that there are no rules because there can be no complete and authoritative statement of a rule. There can be no complete formulation of a rule because, first, rules cannot be self-applying, and, second, they must be adapted to new circumstances. There can be no authoritative statement of a rule because any formulation of a rule must be interpreted anew, and "there are logically any number of rules of law to be derived from any case or series of cases. In addition, because statements in prior judicial opinions are themselves not rules of law but only evidence from which the correct rules may be ascertained . . . there can never be, even momentarily, an authoritative statement of a correct rule of law."[17] Considerations such as these may present some difficulties for the idea that there are rules of law; for if there are such rules, it must be possible to say what they are. This will be discussed in what follows.

THE MOST IMPORTANT REALIST ARGUMENTS
AGAINST RULES

We have thus far examined and challenged several realist criticisms of the view that there are rules in a legal system. In this part we will attempt to meet the most serious difficulties that these criticisms raise.

What exactly are legal rules supposed to be like, such that realists find them objectionable? Putting together suggestions culled from various realist sources, we can characterize a rule as a statement or proposition that (1) exists some place, (2) tells people what they must do or avoid doing (or whatever), (3) is binding on judges, such that (4) there is a correct result to be reached in court cases that is (5) in all cases clearly and unequivocally indicated by the statement or proposition. The arguments against the existence of rules are arguments against the presence

of one or more of these characteristics, all of which are thought
to be required in order for there to be rules. The fourth characteristic is the most important, for if the correct-result requirement
can be shown to be non-problematic, then the objections to the
view that judges are bound (where this is understood as relating
to what is required of judges, and not to their power) disappear.

To begin with, at least for many written laws and probably for
many judicial decisions, there is a central or core interpretation
that will, in non-problematic cases, require a certain legal result.[18]
As an example, consider the old chestnut in which a statute prohibits vehicles from parks; there may be some doubt whether
go-carts are excluded from the park, but there is no doubt when
it comes to cars, trucks, and motorcycles. It is to no avail to reply
that such easy cases never find their way into courts; that only
testifies to everyone's agreement on what the law requires, and
in any event if such a case ever got into court, the judge would
certainly be required to make the obvious decision (unless the
law is being challenged on constitutional or other grounds). If
the realist were to reply that, should the judge fail to give the
required result, the law of the case, so to speak, would be what the
judge, not the statute, said, he could do so only at the expense
of entirely losing his grip on the notions of correct and incorrect,
right and wrong, proper and improper, judicial decisions. The possibility of evaluating judicial decisions at all depends on the
possibility of some decisions being correct and others incorrect.[19]
Indeed, the possibility of thinking of a legal system as a whole as
being justified depends on the possibility of correct results.

The realist might reply that even if there is, in central or core
cases, a correct result, this does not go very far toward showing
that such a notion is applicable in hard cases. In such cases, it is
often said, there are no objective standards for judicial decisions,
and it is here that the judicial art comes into full play. It seems to
me, however, that even here the notion of a correct result has an
important place. To get at this, though, it will be helpful to look
at a few of the notions of objectivity that are sometimes employed
in the denial that there are objective standards for decision in hard
cases. It has been suggested that standards for judicial decision

are objective only if they make it impossible for judges to reach whatever results they want. However, such a view of objectivity is mistaken. On this view decisions are objective only if judges lack power; but to the contrary, being objective or applying objective standards is quite compatible with having the power to do otherwise. Another view of objectivity appears to confuse it with infallibility: standards are objective only if, by applying them, one could not reach an incorrect result.[20] But, again, this view is mistaken. Science is our paradigm of objectivity, but no one would suggest that scientists are not appropriately objective even when it turns out that they are in error. No doubt a discipline and its standards are thought of as being more objective the more likely it is that correct results can be reached; and no doubt science is more objective in this sense, but we need not on this ground give up the enterprise of assessing judicial decisions—i.e. of regarding certain decisions as better than others even in hard cases.

The realist seems to confuse the question of whether there are objective standards and correct results with the skeptical question of whether we can be sure that our standards and our legal results are correct ones. Such skepticism seems appropriate enough; that intelligent people can reach different conclusions must make us wonder at least whether our own standards and conclusions are correct. But they should not make us wonder whether it makes sense to speak of correct results; we could not even wonder sensibly whether our own legal conclusions are correct if there could be no such thing as a correct conclusion. It is important to note that in making these points we need not rely on the possibility of uniquely correct results. For in order to establish the objectivity of legal judgments all that is needed is the possibility that some legal results can be better than others by virtue of having weightier reasons supporting them. As soon as this possibility is acknowledged, however, it is but a short step to acknowledging that some result might be such that the reasons supporting it are weightier than the reasons supporting *any* other decision.

The realist might argue in reply that none of this is any help, for (1) it shows at best that there can be a range of correct results, such that anything outside that range is incorrect and anything inside it is *a* (but perhaps not *the*) correct result; (2) there remains the question of what counts as a reason and what good reasons and the best reasons are; and (3) it is still true that we cannot, very often anyway, be certain of the decisions in hard cases. All of these arguments seem to have some truth in them, but the question is what their implications are. To raise the second problem—of ascertaining what counts as a reason, and as good or the best reasons—is merely to reraise all of the supposed difficulties raised against the notion of correct results. And the reply is the same as before: that we must acknowledge that there can be reasons, and better or worse reasons, if we are to evaluate legal decisions at all, and the fact that we may be uncertain about what the reasons, or the best reasons, in a case are does not mean there are none. But, then, what about the third point? Does not our lack of certainty about which results or reasons are the right ones have implications for judicial decision-making? But what could such implications be? Such skepticism cannot justify a judge's acting arbitrarily. The expected answer to the question "Who is to say what is correct in such matters?" is supposed to imply that one result or opinion is as good as any other. But whatever truth there is in this, it cannot have any implications for judicial decision-making or for judicial theory, for there is all the difference between the judicial attitude that it does not matter what result is reached, and the attitude that we must try, as best we can, to get the right answer, even though we often cannot be sure we have done so.

This leads us to the realist's argument, above—that there is no uniquely correct result, but at best only a range of equally good ones. Now it must be acknowledged that in some cases the considerations for and against different results seem so evenly balanced that one result appears to be no better than another; and it may even be that the balance is so even there *is* no best result.* Do we have in this a refutation of rules, inasmuch as bindingness

* Rolf Sartorious argues otherwise in his article "Social Policy and Judicial Legislation," *American Philosophical Quarterly*, 8 (1971): 158. In his view there is always a single result that "coheres best with the total body of authoritative legal standards." See also his "The Justification of the Judicial Decision," *Ethics*, 78 (1968).

has partially run out? Let us try to answer this by asking what an appropriate—or better, an inappropriate—judicial attitude would be in such a case. A judge would be regarded as acting improperly if he were to say "The considerations are so evenly balanced in this case that I have arbitrarily decided to rule in this way rather than that." But perhaps the impropriety of such a remark would be due not to what is said, but to the saying of it. Some writers have said that the decision in such a case is and must be arbitrary, and that the judge may even be aware that this is so, as in our illustration. But, they argue, a judge must not *say* so because there is value in preserving the myth that judges find law rather than make it.* Suppose, then, that we were to accept the possibility that at some point in judicial decision-making arbitrariness is inevitable. Would this color the entire judicial process in the same way? No, it would not. Would it show that there is no such thing as a correct result? No. Would it, finally, show that there are no rules in a legal system? Again, no.

What of the other important features of rules, as characterized at the beginning of this section—that they exist some place, and that they indicate clearly and unequivocally, in all cases, what is to be done or not done? The latter (the completeness requirement) is clearly too strong a requirement, for there is probably nothing of any interest that could satisfy it; and in any event there is no reason for taking this as involved in the concept of a rule. Rules being clear and unequivocal in their central or core areas, it seems to be a mistake to go on to insist that they really do not exist if they are not clear and unequivocal in *all* cases.

These points aside, however, there is still the question of how the content of rules is to be ascertained. The problem, I gather, is that though there is supposed to be only one rule of law on a given matter, there are many sources for determining what this

---

* Louis L. Jaffe (*English and American Judges as Lawmakers*, Oxford, Eng., 1969, pp. 6–8) attributes such an argument to Lord Radcliffe. Radcliffe is quoted (from *The Law and Its Compass;* 1960) as saying that "judges will serve the public interest better if they keep quiet about their legislative function." See also Paul J. Mishkin, "Foreword: The 1964 Supreme Court Term," *Harvard Law Review,* 79 (1965): 62ff.

rule is, and these may be in conflict or at any rate not clear about what the rule is. This is the problem of authoritativeness we considered in discussing the twelfth realist argument. Now if this is supposed to be a different problem from the simple vagueness of rules, it must be that the sources do not permit the formulation of a rule that is clear even for central or core cases. This could happen, for example, if a statute is inconsistent, or expressed in language so unclear that it is not at all apparent what is being said, or if judicial decisions contradict one another, or if the clear language of a statute is completely contrary to acknowledged legislative intent, or if it is not clear what a prior decision is precedent for. Whatever is to be done in cases of this sort, the question we are concerned with is what this implies for the existence of rules. Problems are presented for rule theories only if there is reason to hold that *law* exists in such cases, but that *rules* do not. But none of these cases do yield this result. Whatever a non-rule theorist says about them, a rule theorist can also say, and with equal plausibility. This leads one to suspect that as far as legal rules and legal theory are concerned the important issues are bindingness and the possibility of correct decisions, not the question of whether the existence of rules implies that the rules of law must always be unambiguously identifiable. That we sometimes cannot identify any rule of law (due to some of the problems mentioned above) does not imply that there are no rules of law at all, though it might imply that on occasion, despite the existence of statutes and prior decisions, there is no rule of law where there is supposed to be one.

There seems, though, to be a different problem lurking behind the idea that if there are rules at all, they must be complete and authoritatively (i.e. infallibly) identifiable; and this problem is of a metaphysical sort. The problem seems to reside in an uneasiness that comes from saying rules exist, for saying they exist seems to imply that they must exist somewhere, and rules apparently do not exist anywhere—all that exists that we can find are statutes, past decisions, and the like. This ontological problem should not be thought troublesome for present purposes, however, whatever one's view on the existence of abstract entities. For even if one thinks that rules of law are abstract entities, which, like numbers and songs, exist without existing anywhere, one need not think that only correct or valid or applicable rules of law exist. That is, the ontological situation need not be thought to have any implications for the question of what decisions judges should make. The judicial art can be thought of as being aimed not at determining what rules of law exist, but rather at determining which (existing) rules are valid. Thus, where I have, in many places, spoken of the existence of a rule of law, we would speak instead of the validity of a rule of law. To avoid some confusions about such an ontological framework, three points should be made. First, that some rule of law is valid or applicable does not imply that it is so from all time, as it were; validity or applicability is determined by human beings.* Second, that a rule of law is valid at one time does not mean that it must remain so; rules of law can cease to be valid. Third, that rules of law exist does not imply that the valid rules are perfectly clear and unambiguous, though lack of these properties may indicate the desirability of refinements that make it clearer which rule or rules are applicable.

In characterizing legal realism, Llewellyn gives the following as a commonly held view among realists: "Distrust of traditional legal rules and concepts insofar as they purport to *describe* what either courts or people are actually doing. Hence the constant emphasis on rules as 'generalized predictions of what courts will do.'"[21] What is revealed here is a fallacy in some realist thinking. The assumption seems to be that if a legal system is taken to be a set of rules or even to consist partly of rules, this implies that in referring to these rules we have thereby described what people and courts actually do. Noting that not all rules as written are followed, and noting especially that courts do not always apply existing rules but interpret, modify, and even reject existing rules, realists conclude that purported legal rules do not describe what actually happens, and hence there are no rules.

---

* This is the legal positivists' credo, at any rate.

But the assumption is mistaken. In saying that a legal system contains rules we refer not to actual behavior, but to the directives according to which citizens and officials *are to* act. Even this, however, is a red flag to some realists, for to say that judges are to act in certain ways is to say that they are *bound* to act in such ways, and the same facts referred to above—that judges interpret, modify, and even reject existing rules—are thought to show that judges are not bound to act in certain ways. This position and the arguments for it have been assessed in this chapter. But we have yet to give an account of a legal system as a set of directives according to which citizens and officials are to act, and in particular of whether, and how, judges are in the appropriate sense bound to act in certain ways but not in others. These matters will be taken up in the next few chapters.

3

Legal Theory and Legal Sociology

In the preceding chapter we noted the inadequacies of legal realism as a theory of law. Yet, as I pointed out in Chapter 1, there is much to be applauded in legal realism. This suggests that legal realists are not trying only (and some perhaps not at all) to give a theory of law, and that what is of value in legal realism is unconnected with legal theory. But then the question arises: What is a theory of law? What is such a theory trying to accomplish? This chapter will focus on these and related questions. In the two succeeding chapters the views of some writers who have theorized in what I believe to be the appropriate way about law will be examined. It will be helpful, though, in discussing the nature of legal theory, to introduce concepts found in some legal theories— such as H. L. A. Hart's concept of a social rule and the concept of validity. Introducing these concepts prior to the more comprehensive discussion of the theories in which they are embedded should cause no particular difficulties.

The results of quite different kinds of legal study might properly be called theories or philosophies of law. Such studies might be wholly descriptive or wholly prescriptive, or some combination of these. On the prescriptive side we can identify a type of study that is sometimes called normative jurisprudence. A legal theory of this sort would presumably be grounded in ethical theory, and might attempt to provide a comprehensive set of principles for use in judicial decision-making.[1] Or such a study might have the more modest aim of making recommendations on ways the judicial process could be improved so as to make it less arbitrary, less prone to manipulation by private interests, or less open to outright dishonesty by officials.[2] Again, if someone were to argue for a doctrine of precedent according to which later decisions have more weight than earlier ones, or for a doctrine of statutory interpretation according to which the intentions of the drafters of a statute have less weight than the interpretations of statutes that promote contemporary social aims, or for some degree of judicial activism or conservatism, such a person would be giving a theory or philosophy of law, or part of one. Interest in this normative sort of philosophizing is evident, for example, in Wolfgang Friedmann's *Legal Theory*. He says, criticizing Hart's legal philosophy, that it would be desirable for a philosophy of law to "indicate directions"; and in the course of criticizing Hans Kelsen he says that "the pure theory of law ... refuses to give any guidance for the solution of ... conflicts [between alternative ideologies]."[3]

Sociological jurisprudence, which is closely connected with legal realism, is concerned with some of these normative pursuits. As indicated in Chapter 1, one of the concerns of the sociological jurisprudents is to identify the individual, social, and public interests at stake in a case, and to reach a decision on the basis of an explicitly recognized social policy that takes these interests into account. But sociological jurisprudence is also closely connected with the sociology of law, the aims of which are wholly descriptive.* What I want to bring out in the following discussion is that though legal realism is in part descriptive sociology, its tools are inadequate for giving a satisfactory descriptive account of law and legal institutions. It will be a central claim of this chapter that a philosophical account or theory of law, or at least a significant part of one, provides the framework for an adequate general sociology of law. A philosophical theory of law (i.e. general jurisprudence) tells us in part what basic items the central terms of an

---

* Some legal sociologists, however, do not keep their sociology and their assessments of legal policy distinct from one another. On this, see Donald J. Black, "The Boundaries of Legal Sociology," *Yale Law Journal*, 81 (1972). See also Alf Ross, *On Law and Justice* (Berkeley, Calif., 1958), pp. 5, 249ff.

adequate sociology of law must refer to. Such a theory of law is not, however, limited to use in sociology. It also provides a framework within which those involved in legal processes are to understand what they do, and within which both practitioners and critics are to appraise what happens. Nevertheless, it will be much clearer what such a theory is like if we approach it from the sociological perspective.

The sociology of law does not consist of any one single thing. That is, though all legal sociology views law as an empirical phenomenon, to be examined by the techniques of the social sciences, different legal sociologists have different aims in conducting their investigations. Some legal sociologists are interested in assessing the "legal effectiveness" of various laws, policies, judicial decisions, and institutions.[4] The purpose of such studies is to disclose the gaps between what should happen, as the law is written (e.g. that suspects in criminal cases are to be apprised of their legal rights), and what in fact happens (e.g. actual police practice).* But this kind of study, which Donald Black calls the "applied sociology of law," though often valuable, is not in his view the "proper concern of legal sociology." That concern, he believes, should be "the development of a general theory of law," an enterprise in which one "seeks to discover the principles and mechanisms that predict empirical patterns of law, whether these patterns occur in this day or the past, regardless of the substantive area of law involved and regardless of the society."[5] Another legal sociologist, however, views even this as a kind of applied sociology— an application of general principles of sociology to social situations in which law plays an important role. As this writer sees it, there is no legal sociology as a special discipline separate and distinct from general sociology, any more than there is a legal logic that is

---

* "Because research in legal sociology consistently shows these disparities, the field has become identified with debunkery and the unmasking of law. In legal scholarship this debunking spirit goes back to the legal realism movement which has haunted law schools since it emerged around the turn of the century. Much legal sociology, then, is a new legal realism, appearing in the prudent garb of social science, armed with sophisticated research methods, new language, and abstract theoretical constructs." (Black, "Boundaries," p. 1087n.)

distinct from the application of general principles of logic to law.[6]

Let us think in terms of a legal sociology that is sufficiently broad to try to characterize a legal system as a whole and perhaps even to discern regularities (sociological laws) that permit the explanation and prediction of at least some legal behavior. What are the phenomena that such a sociology might want to observe and in terms of which it might propose that a legal system be characterized and regularities stated? Different sociologies might take different phenomena as basic. A sociology of law might try to characterize and explain legal phenomena in terms of the observable behavior of people, or in economic terms, or in psychological terms (e.g. drives, gratification, stimulus-response), or in terms of sociological concepts (e.g. elites, establishments, power structures, classes). Correlations might be found, for example, between judicial activity of a certain sort and the economic interests of certain individuals or classes, or between certain kinds of judicial decisions and the psychological profile of the typical judge. Realists, in their social scientific mood, have been very interested in finding correlations of this sort, for such correlations permit the prediction of judicial behavior.

So far there is nothing wrong with sociological studies of the kind just described. Problems do crop up, however, when one insists that sociological accounts of this sort can fully explain legal phenomena. These problems become graver if it is supposed that somehow, in explaining certain legal phenomena solely in psychological, economic, or sociological terms, an account or analysis or explanation has been given of such typically legal concepts as constitution, law, legal system, judgment, citizen, or right, and that there are no important dimensions or aspects of these notions that have not been or cannot be accounted for by means of the terms employed in the sociology in question. It is just this move that some legal realists and other writers on law have made. Some realists have held that when we refer to laws we are referring only to the behavior of certain individuals; thus Oliver Wendell Holmes's remark, "The prophesies of what the courts will do in fact . . . are what I mean by the law," and Jerome

Frank's reference to "actual specific past *decisions,* and guesses as to actual specific future *decisions.*"[7] One thing that such views most obviously miss, however, is the normative or prescriptive character of law. A judge, as many writers have pointed out, does not predict what decision he is going to make. Rather, he makes a decision, and in so doing often appeals to the law as justification for that decision. Now I do not mean to claim there is something new in the idea that laws are directives for behavior, including official behavior. The point is rather that this fact has not always been taken seriously enough, that an adequate theory of law cannot ignore it, and that a thoroughgoing realization of this point indicates the direction in which an adequate theory of law must go.

Maurice Mandelbaum, in his paper "Societal Facts," gives an argument against trying to understand the acts of individuals as members of a society wholly in terms of "psychological facts"—facts concerning the thoughts and actions of specific individuals. There are also, he says, "societal facts"—"facts concerning the forms of organization present in a society," and these facts are necessary to a complete understanding of the behavior of people in a society. We cannot, he believes, understand the actions of people in institutional situations without thinking of the institutions as distinct from the individuals who act in accordance with their rules—for that is how people think of institutions when they interact with others in such situations.[8]

Further, if "societal facts are as ultimate as are psychological facts, then those concepts which are used to refer to the forms of organization of a society cannot be reduced without remainder to concepts which only refer to the thoughts and actions of specific individuals." Mandelbaum makes his point by means of the following example. Suppose we want to explain a person's withdrawing money from a bank by presenting a withdrawal slip to a teller. We cannot adequately explain this by saying the person wrote something on a certain piece of paper and handed it to the person behind the counter, who handed him other pieces of paper of a certain sort. (Nor can we explain it adequately by adding the thoughts of the individual—such as the thought that handing the

paper to the person behind the counter will lead him to hand over
other pieces of paper.) This explanation is inadequate because it
fails to refer to the statuses of the individuals involved, and without this it has not been explained why doing certain acts will have
certain consequences only in certain situations. So an adequate
explanation must refer to or assume the concept of a bank teller,
of a depositor, of money, of a legal system, and maybe others. But
these concepts cannot wholly be explained in terms of (i.e. they
are not reducible to) repeated patterns of behavior-cum-thoughts,
for none of them can be completely explained without reference
to other concepts in the group, or to similar ones. Thus, says
Mandelbaum, there are irreducible societal facts and societal concepts, and accordingly the implications for legal theory are clear:
"[T]he legal system itself cannot be defined in terms of individual
behaviour—even the legal realist must distinguish between the
behaviour of judges and policemen and the behaviour of 'just
anyone.'"[9]

Similar points apply to the concept of a rule, which is essential to
understanding social phenomena, but which cannot be understood
merely in terms of regular patterns of behavior. Consider the often
used example of the rules of chess. A move in a game of chess
involves a series of human movements and the resultant movements of certain objects (chess pieces). By observing a large
number of games of chess, regular patterns will be discerned, and
predictions can be made on the basis of these observed regularities. But, first of all, we can scarcely claim that in having found
these regularities we have explained the sense in which chess is
governed by rules, and the way in which the moves of the players
are seen by them as governed by rules—as constituting compelling
reasons for making certain moves and not others. And the existence
of regularities cannot by itself do this, for we cannot infer from the
fact that no chess player has ever, say, moved a pawn three
spaces on one move, that this is contrary to the rules. Second,
though we might actually learn all of the rules of chess by discern-
ing regularities in behavior, we might also have identified other
regularities that do not correspond to the rules of chess, such as

customs among chess players or strategies that chess players have found important in trying to win. Thus, the rules of chess cannot be identified with the regular patterns of behavior of chess players. Plainly, the points made here in connection with chess apply equally to all rule-governed social phenomena, including the law. "Human social life in a community is not a chaos of mutually isolated individual actions. It acquires the character of community life from the very fact that a large number (not all) of individual actions are relevant and have significance in relation to a set of common conceptions of rules."[10]

Reductive accounts of legal phenomena miss the normative character of those phenomena. Indeed, they often try to get rid of this normative dimension in favor of what is (in principle, at any rate) observable. But as we have seen, to suppose that legal phenomena consist wholly in what is (in principle) observable is to miss the real character of these phenomena. Legal institutions, and a great many other social institutions, are not merely groups of particular individuals who go through a variety of observable motions, some of which can be grouped together in that they are alike in certain ways (i.e. are responses to certain kinds of occurrences and have certain kinds of consequences). Rather, these institutions consist of networks of roles and offices, which cannot be reduced to regular patterns of behavior, and which must be referred to in the explanation of legal phenomena. To be sure, not every bit of the behavior of a person who fills a role is to be explained by reference to that role—officeholders do, for example, eat lunch. More to the point, however, is the fact that not every act an officeholder performs in his official capacity is to be explained wholly by reference to the role, for sometimes officials do things they are not authorized to do, and even things they are prohibited from doing. Of course, not every unauthorized act is deliberate; officials can make mistakes about what they are to do. Thus, the explanation of some unauthorized acts may have to refer to the officeholder's beliefs about what his authorization is; but for others quite independent and idiosyncratic motives may be required in the explanation. It is important to note also that the notion of a role is indispensable if such acts are to be construed not merely as deviant (i.e. out of the ordinary) acts—which, given sufficiently extensive corruption, they need not be—but as (perhaps nonmorally) improper.

Legal institutions consist of roles; roles are sets of rules, or norms. Individual laws are likewise rules or norms. So an adequate theory of law must take account of the rules or norms that are among the phenomena of the legal world, and its central terms (such as law, constitution, judge, judgment, citizen, or sovereign) must refer to rules or sets of rules, or else be definable in terms that refer to rules or sets of rules.

RULES OF LAW AND VALIDITY

What is a rule or norm? Rules or norms are kinds of directives. What, then, is a directive?* Directives set out directions for behavior; they indicate how one is to act (or is not to act, or is permitted to act). They provide guides for action; Alf Ross says a directive "presents an *action-idea*."[11] He regards a directive as the content of a speech act that is designed to guide action—i.e. to indicate that an action-idea is "presented as a pattern of behaviour."[12] The speech act might also say why the addressee is to behave in the indicated way (e.g. that it is good advice, or that it will enable him to accomplish what he wants, or that an evil consequence will be avoided, or that morality or law requires it); but often this is not indicated in or by means of the speech act, and must be gathered from the context.

It seems to me, however, that this is to tie the notion of a directive too closely to speech acts, for not all items that give directions for behavior can readily be understood in this way. Customs, technical norms (for example, "If I want to make the hut habitable, I ought to heat it"), and perhaps some laws are not cases in which someone gives a direction to another. In some cases we might

---

* Different philosophers use different terms to refer to the genus and the species. Von Wright uses "norm" for the genus, whose species are rules, prescriptions or regulations, and directives or technical norms (*Norm and Action*, London, 1963, Chap. 1). Alf Ross uses "directive" for the genus, of which norms are species (*Directives and Norms*, London, 1968, *passim*).

regard the society as a whole as in some sense producing the appropriate speech act, but this will not cover technical norms, recipes, and the like. Perhaps the best course is to regard a directive as the content of a *possible* speech act: it is what the content of an appropriate speech act would be. Further, directives formulate courses of action that one can (logically) follow or fail to follow. These directives are to be taken by those to whom they apply as to be complied with if there are suitable reasons for doing so. These reasons, however, are not part of the content of the directive; and though they may accompany the directive, they often must be gleaned from the context (including the source of the directive).

Among the norms to which an adequate theory of law must refer, some might exist only because of more or less widespread practices in the community; following Hart, we will call these social rules. What a social rule is is best seen by contrasting it with the merely habitual behavior of a group. Suppose that everyone in a group or community goes out on Saturday nights. This concurrence of individual behavior might be mere coincidence. Or maybe it is the result of the same kinds of influences: perhaps everyone works very hard during the week and favors this sort of relaxation. But still, we are supposing, each person does it only because he wants to, and no one thinks he is in any way required to do so. That is, no one regards himself as following a rule, or even believes there is a rule that he happens to be acting in accordance with—though each person may "make it a rule" to go out on Saturday night. Contrast this with the situation in which all or most people not only regularly act in a certain way, but think that they and others should do the thing in question (say, remove their hats in church), and are aware that others likewise think this. Further, there are pressures brought to bear in order to discourage possible noncompliance, and criticism and even sanctions are meted out for deviance. All of these, says Hart, are indicators of the existence of a social rule.

An important aspect of social rules, according to Hart, is what he calls the internal point of view. A person who "accepts" a social rule, or takes the internal point of view with respect to it, would express his attitude toward the rule linguistically by saying such things as "I ought to do..." or "You have a duty to..." By contrast, one who takes the external point of view is concerned only with what the consequences of a particular piece of behavior are likely to be. This attitude is expressed by such locutions as "They will do x to you if you...," or "I had better do x, or else..."[13] Those who take the internal point of view are prepared to comply with the rule, to bring pressure for conformity, and to criticize deviance. Using the concept of the internal point of view, we can express the conditions under which a social rule exists as follows: a social rule exists when, and only when, a sufficiently large number of individuals take the internal point of view with respect to a particular directive. It is important to be clear that the existence of a social rule consists wholly in a sufficiently large number of people taking the internal point of view toward some directive. As far as any particular individual is concerned, however, the social rule exists independently of him, and he can decide whether or not to accept it. If a given individual ceases to accept it, it does not cease to exist; but if everyone ceases to accept it, then it does. It is also to be noted that one who takes the external point of view acknowledges the existence, though not the propriety, of the rule.

Social rules are not the only kinds of rules that can in some sense exist in a society. For it is evident that at least some of the rules that are part of a legal system, and that must be referred to in an adequate account of a legal system are not social rules. For example, the rule that the maximum permissible speed on a highway is fifty-five miles per hour did not arise through the practice of the community; it was deliberately created. Likewise the rule, where it is a rule, that a buyer of commercial paper is subject to the defenses that exist against the seller of the paper—this is a rule of the legal system when created and even before it becomes part of the practice of the appropriate part of the community. And sometimes something that must be acknowledged to be a rule of the legal system exists as such in the face of a significant part of the community *not* adhering to it—for example, rules proscribing the use of marijuana and the performance of certain kinds of sexual acts.

Not all of a society's norms, whether created norms or social norms, are norms of its legal system. A legal theory must therefore delimit its scope by showing how the legal system distinguishes its rules from other norms. What is needed for this purpose is the notion of a *valid* norm of a legal system—i.e. the notion of a norm being a part of a legal system because it satisfies certain authoritative criteria.*

LEGAL AND NONLEGAL NORMS

The central place that the notion of validity and the rules that specify the criteria for validity play in a legal system will be pursued at greater length in the next chapter, when Hart's theory of law is examined. Certain matters, however, can be taken up at this point. As has been pointed out, there must be criteria for distinguishing a society's legal norms from its other norms, and also for determining whether something that is claimed (say, by a lawyer) to be a norm of the legal system, whether or not it is an existing social norm, really is a norm of the legal system. Now if *a, b,* and *c* are the criteria in question, there must be a norm of the legal system that establishes them as the criteria by prescribing that all and only the norms that satisfy *a, b,* and *c* impose legal requirements or are to be given legal effect. This norm, which supplies the criteria in virtue of which norms other than itself belong to a legal system, must be either a created or a non-created norm. But if it is a created norm, then there must be another norm that confers authority on someone who created it. This other norm—is it a created or a non-created norm? If created, then . . . Eventually we must come to a non-created norm, one that itself might not satisfy the criteria it specifies. The upshot, then, is that the norm supplying the criteria of validity either is or rests on a non-created norm. If we suppose, for now, that the non-created norm in question is

---

* Ross distinguishes propositions *about* the law from propositions *of* the law, and points out that all propositions of the former kind involve the notion of validity (*On Law and Justice,* pp. 9–11).

a social norm, then we reach the conclusion that every legal system must include at least one social norm.

Now the question that naturally arises is, what makes *this* social norm a *legal* norm? That is, does or does not the notion of validity apply to this norm? There is no practical problem here; we see readily that it is a legal rule in the sense that it has, and should have, force within the legal system.* But there is a theoretical problem. Let us put the question more broadly: How are we to distinguish law from non-law? That is different from the question of how we distinguish in *particular* cases between actual and putative legal norms, which is determined by the legal system's criteria of validity. The question here is what makes a given set of norms the *law* of a society; what makes us call it law and thereby distinguish it from other norms and normative systems in a society?†

It is not clear (to me, at any rate) whether this is an especially important theoretical question, but since it has been of some concern to legal philosophers, let us go into it briefly. An influential view of the difference between legal and nonlegal norms holds that legal norms are connected in some way with force.[14] For John Austin, for example, laws are commands of the sovereign that are backed up by the threat of force. Hans Kelsen and, following him, Alf Ross and other Scandinavian legal theorists have held that Austin's account of legal norms is defective. Yet in their own accounts they too maintain a connection between law and force. Law is not, according to Ross, a body of rules "upheld by force," but a body of rules "concerning the exercise of [physical] force."[15] And Kelsen says: "A rule is a legal rule not because its efficacy is secured by another rule providing for a sanction. The problem of coercion

---

* As we shall see in Chapter 4, however, there is not only theoretical but also practical difficulty when it comes to the question of exactly what the content of this rule is.

† Joseph Raz appears to run some of these questions together when he says that John Austin, Hans Kelsen, and H. L. A. Hart were trying "to formulate a test that would enable them to determine whether any two laws belong to the same legal system or not." See his "The Identity of Legal Systems," *California Law Review*, 59 (1971): 796. Better would be "what makes any two norms belong to the same system of norms?," which is different from "what makes a system of norms the *legal* system of a society?"

(constraint, sanction) is not the problem of securing the efficacy of rules, but the problem of the content of rules."[16] For example, instead of a law that says to citizens that murder is prohibited and another that directs some official to impose a sanction on violators, there is, on Kelsen's view, only one rule—roughly, that if someone commits a murder, then official *O* ought to impose a sanction on him. This directive is addressed to the official, not to citizens. The law, according to Kelsen, imposes duties on officials, and only on officials, and citizens determine what they are to do by looking at the conditions under which officials are to impose sanctions.

Whatever advantages, if any, Kelsen's view has over Austin's, neither view is satisfactory unless there is the required connection between law and force.* If we assume all law is state law, then Austin's and Kelsen's view of the connection between law and force is related to the Weberian definition of the state as that entity within a geographical area having a monopoly of the use of force. Though there is undoubtedly some connection between the state (and its law) and the use of force, Weber's characterization of the state is far from unambiguous, and there does not seem to be any reading of it on which it is true. First of all, the state is obviously not the only institution to have used force in the past, or even to use it at present, and so the state cannot be defined as the only institution actually using force. In the second place, to say the state is the only institution having the *legal right* to use force, and then to say it is this that distinguishes the state and its law from other institutions and nonlegal norms is to argue circularly. Further, the state is not the only institution that claims to use force legitimately (where legitimacy is not merely a matter of legal entitlement). And finally, the state is not in fact the only

---

* Kelsen's view is really no better than Austin's in accounting for official duty, for on both views officials have assigned tasks but no legal duty to carry them out. Furthermore, Kelsen is mistaken in his contention that citizens can infer what they are to do from instructions to officials to mete out certain kinds of undesirable treatment in certain circumstances. As Hart points out (*The Concept of Law*, Oxford, Eng., 1961, p. 39), Kelsen's view does not allow for the distinction between a tax and a fine. See Chapter 7, below.

institution that uses force legitimately; people have, for example, the right to use physical force to defend themselves, and parents may physically punish their children for violating rules that they have laid down (and these rules, despite the presence of the sanction, are not laws). Naturally, it is not the case that these uses of force are legitimate just because permitted (or at least not prohibited) by the law.

What has been argued thus far is that the distinction between legal and nonlegal norms cannot be made solely in terms of a connection between law and force, for some nonlegal norms and institutions have a similar connection. There are also problems going in the other direction: some legal norms have no connection with force. Violations of legal norms might, for example, result in fines that require no force for their collection, or in the loss of expected benefits such as welfare payments, or in the revocation of a license, or in the loss of the right to vote. Furthermore, though I shall not argue the point here, it is not so certain that all legal norms are even connected with sanctions, let alone force. Removing a corrupt official from office may be, but need not be, a sanction for misbehavior. Similarly in the case of deporting an alien on the basis of moral character.*

A second view of the distinction between legal and nonlegal norms holds that legal norms are connected with quite complex social arrangements involving roles and offices—that is, legal norms are institutionalized whereas nonlegal norms are not. More particularly, the claim is that there are institutions for creating and especially for applying those norms that count as legal norms.[17] However, though this may be a necessary feature of legal norms, other sets of norms in a society might likewise be institutionalized. One might then say that law is the most pervasive set of institutionalized norms in a society. But other sets of norms could turn out to be equally or more pervasive, for example in a society in which the church is strong and the state relatively weak. The law might then be identified as that set of norms connected with the state (the political system); the law might be identified with the

* These points are pursued in greater detail in Chapter 7.

state, or might be viewed as a subset of the political norms of a society. But then the problem of representing law as distinct from other sets of norms depends (1) on how the state is to be characterized (and thus distinguished from other social institutions), and (2) either on there being only one set of institutionalized norms connected with a state, or, if more than one, on there being a way of distinguishing legal institutions from these other institutions. We seem to have returned to where we were at the beginning of this brief inquiry. Perhaps a way can be found to characterize the state and to make the distinction between legal and nonlegal norms and institutions; but it may be that in the end there is no theoretically satisfactory way of making these distinctions.

DEFINITION AND THEORY

A theory of law, we have said, is an account of normative phenomena and normative structures. But a theory of law, as it has thus far been characterized, does not itself make any normative claims. It gives a description, not an evaluation, of normative phenomena. Some writers, however, have held that a theory of law can be only partly descriptive—which is to say, that an adequate theory of law cannot be ideology-free. A. M. Honoré forcefully expresses this point of view in the following passage:

Legal theory may be looked at from two different points of view. On the one hand it may be thought of as the enterprise of describing the conditions which must exist in order that there may be laws and of giving an account of the characteristics of laws. On the other hand it can be conceived as the advocacy of political and moral ideals within the framework of a convention which requires them to be put forward as versions of the meaning, definition, or function of law. Legal theorists are engaged in a form either of cartography or of ideological warfare.

In the last resort it is the second of these points of view which more closely resembles the truth. Even when they lay an elaborate smokescreen to disguise their emplacements the legal theorists are committed. This is and must be so so long as the notion of law is intimately linked with that of obedience. When we say that something is a law we are, among other things, striking a special posture towards the question whether it should be obeyed, and, if it is disobeyed, how that disobedience is to be justified. A theory of law is, *inter alia,* a theory about the appropriate attitudes of obedience and disobedience to certain prescriptions, and it would be less than candid to pretend that such a theory can be morally or politically neutral. Legal theory is a form of practical reason, not a science. In contrast with law-making and law reform, which can in theory be scientific to the same extent as other goal-determined techniques like medicine, legal theory is in the end an elaborate form of exhortation or an elaborate display of commitment.[18]

In contrast to Honoré, Hart, in his "Definition and Theory in Jurisprudence," animadverts on definitions of legal concepts that commit us to a theory. The theories that various definitions of legal concepts lead to, according to Hart, fall into "a familiar triad": (1) that legal terms refer to actual or likely behavior of certain individuals; (2) that they refer to ideal or fictitious entities; and (3) that they refer to real but invisible entities. One reason Hart finds such definitions suspect is that they seem to warrant certain legal outcomes, such as that a corporation cannot commit a crime or maintain a lawsuit because it is not a person.

It is of course clear that the assertion that corporate bodies are real persons and the counterassertion that they are fictions of the law were often not the battle cries of analytical jurists. They were ways of asserting or denying the claims of organized groups to recognition by the State. But such claims have always been confused with the baffling analytical question "What is a corporate body?" so that the classification of such theories as Fiction or Realist or Concessionist is a criss-cross between logical and political criteria.[19]

Part of what Hart tells us to avoid seems to be just what Honoré tells us cannot be avoided in legal theory. Our question, then, is whether we can devise a definition (or descriptive theory—hereafter "D-theory") of law that does not commit us to some normative theory (hereafter "N-theory") of law, and in particular whether the kind of theory referred to earlier in this chapter must have normative commitments.

Undoubtedly there is some connection between a D-theory of law and claims (of a certain sort) about what is to be done, for a D-theory of law tells us how to determine which norms are valid legal norms. However, to be given this information is not yet to be told how to behave or how to decide a case, any more than a D-theory of chess tells us either to play chess or to play by its rules, let alone by its principles and strategies. With chess it is moral principles that tell us to follow the rules, and it is usually only our desire to play that gives us reason to play. In chess the only connection between a D-theory and what we are to do is conditional: if you are playing chess, here is how to determine what rules are to be followed. Similar points apply to the law. Moral principles, not a D-theory, tell us (both citizens and officials) whether we are subject to a legal system, and whether we ought to follow any given rule of a legal system. The only connection between a D-theory of law and what we are to do is the conditional one that if we are to act in accordance with the law, here is how to determine what rules are to be followed.

Jonathan Cohen, responding to Hart in a symposium on Theory and Definition in Jurisprudence, has argued that definitions of legal terms have an effect on legal decisions, that to ask for a definition is often to ask how the term *should* be used (that is, it is a request for a tool to be used, say, in deciding a case), and that a theory-neutral definition is not useful for this purpose and hence is incomplete. The problem of definition, as he sees it, is to provide for word usage in abnormal situations (i.e. to provide a rule or principle to be used in decision-making), and thus to give a definition is to buy in on a theory of judicial decision-making.[20]

When it comes to definitions of such legal terms as right and corporation (and perhaps even law and legal system), Cohen is partially but not wholly correct. A request for a definition of legal right can come at two levels, at each of which it is a request for something different: (1) it can be a request for an account of the concept of a legal right, or (2) it can be a request for standards that determine what rights should be recognized within a legal system. Strictly speaking, only the first is a request for a definition, but as Hart has pointed out, the second is often confused with a request for a definition.

Request (1) can be answered in a normatively neutral way—by

reference (a) to the concepts of a legal system, a valid rule of a legal system, and a legal principle, and (b) to an account of the way in which certain rules and principles of a legal system embody or protect rights. Thus, Hart is close to the mark in the part of his contextual definition of a legal right that says the statement "X has a legal right" is true only if there is a legal system under which there are rules that . . . [21] Request (2), on the other hand, does require a normative answer. It is a question that usually arises and is properly to be answered *within* a legal system in contexts in which rules are being created and interpreted.

4

Law, Rules, and Principles

Legal positivism, in its widest sense, is the view that the study of the nature of law is a study of law as it is, and not of law as it ought to be. There is nothing objectionable, according to positivists, in discussing the merits of laws and suggesting reforms; but only from the data on the law as it actually exists in the legal systems of various societies, they say, can one properly theorize about the nature of law. In this broad sense, legal realists are positivists. But in a narrower sense of positivism, legal realism contrasts with positivism in that the proponents of the two positions give different pictures of what legal systems are like. According to positivism, first of all, there is a morally neutral test for determining what the law is. And second, whatever (and only whatever) satisfies this test is law and is thus binding on both citizens and legal officials—including, and especially, judges. Parts of this second aspect of positivism, we have seen, are rejected by realists. Other opponents of positivism have attacked the idea that there is a content-neutral test by which the law can be ascertained. In the contemporary debate, in particular, Ronald Dworkin has attacked H. L. A. Hart's positivistic theory of law on this point. We will here trace the development of positivism from John Austin to Hart, and examine critically Dworkin's argument against Hart.

JOHN AUSTIN'S THEORY OF LAW

John Austin's aim, in his 1832 work, *The Province of Jurisprudence Determined,* is to give an account of positive law. But since there are more kinds of law than positive law, Austin first tries to characterize the notion of law (that is, law "properly so called," which is distinct from morals and from other things that are called laws improperly or not in the strict sense) and then to distinguish positive law from other kinds of law. A law in the proper sense, says Austin, is a species of command; a command, he says, is a signification of desire (or the expression or intimation of a wish), directed by one rational being to another, concerning something that the latter is to do or refrain from doing, and backed up by a threat of evil to be imposed if the wish is not complied with. In short, a command is a directive backed by a threat; its form is "Do *x*, and if you don't, evil *e* will be imposed on you."

Even before we go on to complete Austin's account of a law, we are in a position to go into some greater detail about the position thus far outlined. For one thing, command and duty are, according to Austin, correlative terms. If someone is liable to be harmed by someone else in case he fails to comply with that person's wishes, he is bound or obliged to comply; hence, a duty is imposed on him, which he violates if he disobeys the command. The threatened evil for noncompliance is called a sanction, and wherever there is a sanction in the offing there is a command and thus a duty. Accordingly, the notions of a command, a duty, and a sanction are connected. Austin maintains that each of these terms "is the name of the same complex notion"; "each of the three terms *signifies* the same notion but each *denotes* a different part of that notion, and *connotes* the residue."[1] The complex idea referred to by each term is "A wish conceived by one, and expressed or intimated to another, with an evil to be inflicted and incurred in case the wish is disregarded"; the term command refers directly to the expression of the wish, and indirectly to the duty and the sanction; duty refers directly to the chance of incurring evil and indirectly to the other two; and sanction refers directly to the evil itself, and indirectly to the other two. What Austin gives us, then, is a command theory of law, together with a sanction theory of duty.

There is another important feature of Austin's notion of a command. According to him, the notion of a command implies a relation of superiority and inferiority. Superiority, in his account, has to do with power (or, as he calls it, might); it is the power to enforce compliance with a wish. If I tell you to do something, and back this up with a threat, I have not issued a command unless I can make good my threat. If laws are commands, they must have this feature; the implications for Austin's picture of law and society are obvious.

Thus far we have characterized laws as Austin sees them, but not that subclass of laws with which he is particularly concerned —positive law. For the account of law so far given includes Divine law (if there is any), as well as human law. Positive law, of course, is human law. But we are not yet there, for only some of the directives set by men to men are the law of a society—namely, those that are set by political superiors to political inferiors. Mafia leaders satisfy all of the conditions of law up to this one, but their commands are not the positive law of a society.[2] Who, then, is the political superior (the sovereign) in a society? The sovereign, on Austin's view, is the person (or group of persons) who is habitually obeyed by everyone else (or almost everyone else) in the society, but who habitually obeys no other person or group. That is, the sovereign is internally supreme, and independent.

A law, then, is (1) an expression of a wish, (2) together with a threat of evil for noncompliance, (3) together with the power to enforce compliance, (4) emanating from a person (or group of persons) who alone is habitually obeyed by the bulk of the society and who habitually obeys no one. In giving this account of what a law is, Austin is not stipulating that he is going to treat as laws only what accords with the account; he is claiming that all positive law (in the strict sense) as it is found in existing legal systems does in fact meet his conditions. But Austin does recognize the need for an important amendment, aware that his account does not accord with actual legal systems in one respect. The problem is that not all laws appear to emanate from the will of a sovereign; sometimes customs are properly recognized as law by the courts, but these cannot be thought of as expressions of legislative will. Austin deals with this problem as follows. Custom, he says, is merely part of the positive morality of a society and is not law until it is applied by a court. But the will of some commander or other is still responsible for these laws, for commands can be either express or tacit. Since the legislative will has not spoken against these customs, and since it permits their recognition as law, it assents to their recognition and hence tacitly commands it. Thus, all law does indeed emanate from the will of the sovereign—if not directly (expressly) then indirectly (tacitly).

However clear and initially plausible Austin's theory of law is, there are several critical points to be brought out.[3]

1. The first point is perhaps a small one, and is raised here only to highlight an important feature of Austin's account. Austin defines laws in terms of commands. The notion of a command is most at home in such contexts as the military, where there is a hierarchical arrangement of competence and prerogative, and where commands go from a higher to a lower level. The idea of a command, in its central usages, includes the idea of authority, and hence is already very close to the idea of law. But Austin is supposed to be (among other things) explaining, not presupposing, authority. Austin's actual model is more like the case of a gunman making a demand backed by a threat, than a sergeant giving an order to a subordinate. The picture Austin wants to convey is that of the gunman writ large: an individual (or group) who operates somewhat like a gunman (gives orders backed by threats and has the power to carry out the threats) and is regularly obeyed by most in the society while habitually obeying no one else.

2. Austin's account of law most closely approximates penal statutes, or, more generally, laws that impose duties. But there are other sorts of laws that his account does not seem to fit. First, there are what are sometimes called power-conferring laws or rules of competence. For example, some laws give people the power to make wills or to declare themselves trustees; and others confer power on officials to adjudicate or to legislate. Such laws do not impose duties—they do not require people to do or refrain

from doing certain things. Rather, they make it possible to do certain things that could not be done absent these laws. Second, and similarly, laws that give permissions (e.g. to use self-defense) appear not to conform to Austin's concept of law.

It may be that a least some of the above kinds of laws can be incorporated into an Austinian account of law by treating powers, competences, and permissions as *fragments* of laws, as conditions on which duties, backed by sanctions, are imposed on people (either citizens or officials).[4] For example, if a law (reconstructed and schematically) were to say "If the Federal Power Commission orders someone *s* to do *x*, then *s* shall do *x*, and if he does not, then he is subject to penalty *p*," this imposes a duty on certain people to follow the orders of the FPC, and by implication might be said to confer on the FPC the power to make such orders.

There are a few things to be said about such an attempt to "reduce" a law of this kind to duty-imposing laws. First, even if powers, permissions, and the rest can be treated as fragments of duty-imposing laws, one might wonder whether this really makes a case for saying that all laws, when properly understood, can be seen to impose duties, and whether, if it does, this advances our understanding of the nature of law. In one way, perhaps, such a move makes things simpler, for what appear to be different kinds of laws are now seen as varieties of a single kind of law. But in another way things have become more complex, for our understanding of law will still depend on our having distinguished and explained the different varieties, with the added difficulty that we must perform the task of showing how they are fragments of a single kind of law. Our understanding, in short, is not always advanced by achieving logical simplification. Second, a law expressible in hypothetical form does not necessarily imply a permission, power, or anything else. A law that says "If a taxpayer has income from gambling, he must declare it" may seem to imply that all gambling is permitted, but all gambling is not permitted, even though income from all gambling is taxable. And third, it is not clear that permissions, competences, and powers can always be expressed, or at any rate fully expressed, as sets of laws imposing

duties on certain conditions. Think, for example, of a law conferring power on certain individuals to act as mediators in labor disputes; it is hard to see what duty-imposing laws such a power
could be fragments of. Perhaps, though, such laws can after all be
ingeniously represented as fragments of duty-imposing laws. It
still seems that this would obscure the nature of such laws, and
would not be very illuminating.

3. In most legal systems, including our own, the sovereign is
bound by law. But if laws are orders backed by sanctions, how can
this be so? This self-binding character of law would be possible
on Austin's view only if a person can give himself orders. But
it is not clear that anyone can do this; someone can resolve to
behave in a given way, but that is a different thing. One way to
deal with this is to distinguish different capacities or roles of the
sovereign: his capacity as sovereign and his capacity as citizen.
The idea would be that though a sovereign cannot order himself
in his capacity as sovereign, he can do so in his capacity as citizen.
This seems acceptable, but it is of no avail to Austin, for the
notion of a legal role or capacity involves power-conferring rules,
and these, as we have seen, are problematic for him.

4. A related difficulty is Austin's claim that the legislative
power of the sovereign is unlimited, and necessarily so, whereas
in many legal systems legislative power is in fact limited. If it is
limited by some act of the legislators themselves, the problem is as
above. But it may also be limited, as in our own legal system, by a
written constitution. One way for Austin to deal with this would
be to maintain that in such a case it is not the legislature that is the
sovereign, but the person or persons having the power to alter the
constitution. In the United States the electorate has this power,
and it is indeed sometimes said that in the United States the people
are sovereign. But if the sovereign is the people, then Austin's
conception of law as involving a relation of habitual obedience
between sovereign and subject becomes strained to the breaking
point.

5. Austin's analysis of law does not account for laws governing
the succession of one government by another in a society. On

Austin's view the existence of law depends on the habitual obedience of most of the people in a society to some individual or group
(the sovereign). Thus on Austin's view when, say, a monarch dies,
there is at that point no person commanding the habitual obedience of the rest of the people in the society; hence there is no law in
that society until someone else begins to give orders backed by
sanctions and comes habitually to be obeyed. But though this is
what happens when one government replaces another by revolu-
tion, it is clearly not what happens when there is orderly, law-
governed succession. So Austin cannot account for laws governing
succession, for on his view they, like all laws, cease to exist when
the sovereign dies.

The other side of the problem of continuity is the problem of
the persistence of law. When rulers change, the old law characteristically remains in force until altered by the new ruler. But on
Austin's view the old law ceases to be in force. He tries to deal
with this by saying that the application of the old law by courts is
done with the tacit approval of the new sovereign, and is thus a
tacit expression of his will. But this is implausible; past legislation
does not cease to be law at all, becoming law, in the way that
custom does, only on being applied by the courts.

6. Laws obligate or impose duties on us. Austin maintains that
these notions are connected with the idea of a command: to be
commanded is to be threatened with a sanction and thus to be
placed under a duty.[5] But this seems quite mistaken. It may be
prudent to comply with the orders of a gunman, but there is no
duty to do so; one is perhaps obliged, but not obligated. Thus it
appears that Austin has given what is at best an example of being
obliged, not an account of being obligated. Austin may have been
misled by the idea that laws are binding on citizens, for one notion
of being bound is the notion of being forced or physically constrained or otherwise coerced. But there is also another notion of
being bound, which assumes there are certain legitimate requirements applicable to a person in a particular situation. Obligation
has to do with this notion of bindingness, not the first one. Two
further points serve to bring out the difference between being

obliged and being obligated. First, one can be under an obligation even if there is no chance of being caught and penalized. And second, a statement that someone has or is under a legal obligation functions as a reason or justification for his acting in a certain way and also for the imposition of a sanction if he fails to do so, whereas a statement that someone was obliged to do something is never a justification, but may be an excuse. Austin's account misses these points.

H. L. A. HART'S ADDITIONS TO THE POSITIVIST POSITION

H. L. A. Hart, in his 1961 book, *The Concept of Law,* presents a positivistic account of law that is designed to give a more adequate picture of the notion of law by dealing with the various difficulties besetting Austin's account. At the center of Hart's analysis is the concept of a *rule* and in particular the concept of a social rule, both of which were introduced in the preceding chapter. Before going into greater detail concerning Hart's view of law as consisting of rules, we should see how, by employing the existence of such rules, Hart proposes to deal with the problems facing Austin's account of law. Take, for example, the self-bindingness of law: given Hart's view we need not wonder whether a person can give himself orders; we may think instead of a rule prescribing that officials are bound by the same rules as non-officials. Take the problem of continuity: since social rules can survive the death of a sovereign, succession can be prescribed even when there is no sovereign to whom the people are then obedient; and similarly for the problem of the persistence of law. The problem of different kinds of law is also taken care of, for rules need not take the form of orders; they can create competences and establish permissions. Hart also maintains that obligations can (indeed must) be understood in terms of the existence of rules; for according to him, to say that a person is under an obligation is to "apply such a general rule to a particular person by calling attention to the fact that his case falls under it."[6]

Recalling Hart's notion of a rule and of the internal point of view with regard to rules, let us see what use he makes of these ideas. Hart distinguishes two kinds of rules, the union of which, he says, explains the nature of law. The distinction is between what he calls primary and secondary rules. (Hart often makes it seem in his writings that this distinction is the same as the one between duty-imposing and power-conferring rules; but though the two overlap, they are not the same.[7]) Primary rules are (at least) the duty-imposing rules in a society. Hart asks us to imagine a society that has only rules of this kind—perhaps a primitive society. But it is plain, he says, "that only a small community closely knit by ties of kinship, common sentiment, and belief, and placed in a stable environment, could live successfully by such a regime of unofficial rules. In any other conditions such a simple form of social control must prove defective and will require supplementation in different ways."[8]

There are three defects from which such a community suffers. The first is uncertainty, for in such a community there is no systematic procedure for resolving questions about what the rules of the community are or what their scope is. The second defect is the static quality of the community's rules; change is accomplished only via the slow process of growth and decay; there is no means of making or adopting rules, and no way to alter the positions created by the primary rules. The third defect is inefficiency; the rules are maintained only by diffuse social pressure, and there is no agency that can authoritatively ascertain whether they have been violated.

The remedy for these defects is the supplementation of the primary rules with secondary rules, and herein, says Hart, we see the step from the pre-legal to the legal world. The introduction of remedies for all of these defects is sufficient to bring about a legal system; law can thus profitably be viewed as the union of primary and secondary rules. The remedy for uncertainty is the introduction of a rule of recognition, which authoritatively settles questions about what the rules are and what their scope is. The remedy for the static quality of a system of primary rules is the introduction of rules of change, which empower certain individuals to introduce new primary rules and to eliminate old ones. The remedy for inefficiency is the introduction of rules of adjudication, which among other things confer power to ascertain whether rules have been violated.

Hart's thesis that a rule of recognition exists in every legal system is a central feature of his positivistic theory of law, for it is this, he claims, that distinguishes which things are law and which are not, and that provides a means of identifying the law in a morally neutral way. (The rule of recognition also provides an answer to the question of when a legal system *exists.*[9]) Given the centrality of the rule of recognition, a few more words about it are in order. The problem that such a rule is intended to rectify is uncertainty about what the other rules are and about the scope of any one rule. Think of a game that children might dream up in which they make up the rules as they go along. As the game comes to be played more often, rules become more or less fixed, but disputes may nevertheless arise over what the rules are. Now suppose the players get together and write down the rules on a piece of paper. They have thereby implicitly accepted the secondary rule that the rules of the game are what the paper says they are, and that disputes are to be resolved by looking at the paper. This secondary rule is a rule of recognition. (Note that this rule does not confer any powers, such as legislative powers, on anyone.) The rule of recognition in a legal system is of course more complex, though similar in kind. A simplified version of the rule of recognition in the English legal system, according to Hart, might be that whatever the Queen in Parliament enacts is law. This rule establishes the criteria, the conclusive tests, for what is to count as law in England. Where there is a constitution that is accepted, it is the rule of recognition in that society.[10]

Using the notion of a rule of recognition, we can explain the concept of validity: a law is valid if, and only if, it satisfies the tests provided by the rule of recognition. Something that satisfies these tests is a rule of the system; it has legal existence; it is, in a word, valid.

The rule of recognition is a legal rule and belongs to the legal system. It differs from other rules of the system, though, in that its existence is determined not by criteria laid down in other rules, but rather by the fact that it is actually applied. As Hart puts it, "[W]hereas a subordinate rule of a system may be valid and in that sense 'exist' even if it is generally disregarded, the rule of recognition exists only as a complex, but normally concordant, practice of the courts, officials, and private persons in identifying the law by reference to certain criteria. Its existence is a matter of fact."[11]

Since the existence of a rule of recognition is not open to question but is a matter of empirical fact—that is, a matter primarily of its being accepted by officials—it is quite different from other rules, which may exist (i.e. be valid) even if ignored. Does the notion of validity apply to the rule of recognition? According to the explanation of validity given in the paragraph above, it does not; but we can expand the notion of validity to cover this case. We can say that other rules are valid if, and only if, they pass the test of the rule of recognition, whereas the rule of recognition is valid if, and only if, it exists (i.e. is accepted, primarily by officials). Aphoristically, we might say that whereas the other legal rules are accepted because valid, the rule of recognition alone is valid because accepted.

If the existence of the rule of recognition is an empirical fact (and hence is a social rule), we are brought to the knotty problem of what happens when there is doubt about what the rule of recognition is or how it is to be applied in difficult cases. Take, for example, the case of *Marbury* v. *Madison*,[12] in which the question was whether the Supreme Court had the right to review the content of statutes passed by Congress as well as the right to examine whether or not they were enacted according to the processes prescribed by the Constitution. This was a case in which, Hart acknowledges, the ultimate rule of a legal system (the rule of recognition) was in doubt. The question here is whether anything could possibly count as a good legal reason (a reason prescribed by the law) for resolving such a case in one way rather than in another, or whether, on the other hand, it cannot be resolved by any legal means at all, but must rather await general acceptance by the officials of one solution or another. Hart answers this question by acknowledging that at some point we may just run out of law to apply, and that there may be no legal justification for such a judicial decision. It may be a mistake, he says, to think

that every step taken by a court is covered by some general rule conferring in advance the authority to take it, so that its creative powers are *always* a form of delegated legislative power. The truth may be that, when courts settle previously unenvisaged questions concerning the most fundamental constitutional rules, they *get* their authority to decide them accepted after the questions have arisen and the decision has been given. Here all that succeeds is success.[13]

However, according to Hart, the fact that there may come a point when there are cases to decide and no grounds prescribed by the legal system for deciding them is not particularly worrisome. The areas of judicial decision-making in which the exercise of discretion is unavoidable are fairly restricted, and in any event this discretion is usually limited in several ways, as will be indicated shortly.

We may now attempt to summarize some of Hart's most important ideas about law. Two central concepts and a methodological aid characterize Hart's philosophizing about law. The concepts are the concept of a social rule with its internal aspect and the concept of the rule of recognition. As a methodological aid Hart asks us to look at law not merely from the point of view of the recipient—the citizen to whom duty-imposing laws are directed. Rather, he asks us to pay attention also to the officials in a legal system: how they operate under and with the rules and what point of view they take toward the rules.

Hart's view is that we cannot understand important legal concepts like obligation, rights, validity, competence, sanction, and legislation unless we pay attention to the internal aspect of social rules, to the way in which people use rules as standards for their own behavior and the behavior of others. Obligation and duty are to be explained by referring to the internal aspect of primary rules; validity, legal powers, capacities, and other concepts are to be explained by referring to the internal aspect of secondary and/or power-conferring rules, and in particular to the point of view taken by officials. It is in this way that Hart claims to deal satisfactorily with the problems in Austin's account of law: Austin's problem of continuity is a problem of legal capacities; his problem with persistence is a problem of validity; his problem with the limitedness of the sovereign is a problem of competences and powers; and so on.

Hart's analysis of law in terms of rules gives us a picture of a legal system as a system of rules, the unity of the system being due to the rule of recognition. In this picture the validity of each law refers back to some other rule that authorizes an official or an official body to establish that law, and so on until the rule of recognition is reached. We thus have the picture of a legal system as a network of chains of validity, all of which trace back to the rule of recognition; and the rule of recognition, together with all of these chains, constitutes the legal system of a society. Rules that cannot be traced back to the rule of recognition are not part of the system—are not laws—even if in many ways they seem to be.[14] (Whether these directives should be viewed as laws and what a person's obligation is with respect to such "laws" will be touched on in Chapter 6.)

There is one further aspect of Hart's positivism that must be brought out. This concerns judicial decision-making. Court cases are decided, in Hart's model, by ascertaining what the law is (via the rule of recognition) and applying it to the facts of the case. Hart is aware, though, that things are not always this simple, for sometimes cases arise that are not clearly covered by any of the rules of law. This is due, in large measure, to what he calls the "open texture of law," the "penumbral" areas in every rule of law where it is not clear what the rule requires, or whether it applies at all in borderline cases. In cases of this sort, Hart says, judges have a limited discretion to decide whether the rule is to be applied or not. This discretion is limited by some sense of the point of the rules as revealed in their central and nonproblematic applications. But since judicial decisions must be made even when guidance from within the law is lacking, judicial discretion must be conceived, in positivism, as permitting judges to look outside the law for standards to guide them in supplementing old legal rules or creating new ones.

RONALD DWORKIN ON PRINCIPLES OF LAW

In a series of articles dating back to the 1960's Ronald Dworkin has mounted a forceful attack against some of the central aspects of Hart's theory of law, and against three ideas in particular: that the law of a community is a set of rules that can be identified by means of a master social rule; that in deciding hard cases judges must get guidance from extralegal standards; and that having a legal obligation is a matter of a valid legal rule applying to a person in certain circumstances. All of these seem to be related to a central tenet of Dworkin's—namely, he denies that everything that is part of a legal system, that has legal weight, and that judges must take into consideration in deciding cases is a rule of law. In short, there are other things in a legal system besides rules:

> [W]hen lawyers reason or dispute about legal rights and obligations, particularly in those hard cases when our problems with these concepts seem most acute, they make use of standards that do not function as rules, but operate differently as principles, policies, and other sorts of standards. Positivism . . . is a model of and for a system of rules, and its central notion of a single fundamental test for law forces us to miss the important roles of these standards that are not rules.[15]

What are "principles, policies, and other sorts of standards," and how do they differ from rules? (Though principles and policies are different, we will consider explicitly only principles.) A principle is "a standard that is to be observed . . . because it is a requirement of justice or fairness or some other dimension of morality."[16] "No one shall be permitted to profit from his own fraud, or to take advantage of his own wrong" is a principle. This is substantially different, in Dworkin's view, from a rule, an example of which is: "The maximum legal speed on the turnpike is fifty-five miles an hour." Rules, he says, "are applicable in an all-or-nothing fashion. If the facts a rule stipulates are given, then either the rule is valid, in which case the answer it supplies must be accepted, or it is not, in which case it contributes nothing to the decision." Rules "set out legal consequences that follow automatically when the conditions provided are met." Principles do not have these features. Rather, a principle "states a reason that argues in one direction, but does not necessitate a particular decision"; and principles "have a dimension that rules do not—the dimension of weight or importance."* Thus sometimes the law does in fact permit people to profit from their legal wrongs. For example, if one person occupies and openly uses another's land for a sufficiently long period of time, he may come thereby to own the land (this is the doctrine of adverse possession); and there are other examples in the law. But these legal doctrines do not mean that the principle that no one may profit from his own wrong is not a principle of law at all. It is certainly a legal consideration, one that judges must take into account in deciding certain cases, but that might be outweighed by other principles (or perhaps, though this is contentious, by social policies). One of the best-known cases in which it was held that this principle did have sufficient weight was cited earlier: the case of *Riggs* v. *Palmer,* in which the defendant's right to inherit under the will of the man he murdered was challenged. The court pointed out that though the legal rules governing the matter would give the inheritance to Palmer, the principle cited above, which the court referred to as one of the "general, fundamental maxims of the common law,"[17] controlled the operation of the legal rule, and consequently held that Palmer was not entitled to the inheritance.

Before we proceed to the central aspects of Dworkin's attack on Hart, it should be made clear that though a weighing is required where principles are involved, there can be no "rules" prescribing how much weight a principle is to have in a given case. This is an area where judges must exercise discretion, and

* The distinction between rules and principles may not be as sharp as Dworkin suggests; the difference may be one of degree and not of kind. See J. M. Eekelaar, "Principles of Revolutionary Legality," in A. W. B. Simpson, ed., *Oxford Essays in Jurisprudence* (2d series; Oxford, Eng., 1973), pp. 30–37. However, Eekelaar points out, none of this shows that there is not an important distinction to be drawn between rules and principles—namely, with regard to their origins.

in which the highest judicial virtues may be displayed. What is sometimes called judicial creativity comes in at such points. It is important to remember, however, that though judges reach these decisions largely as a result of their own estimates of the weight of relevant principles (and, indeed, must often rely largely on their own resources to determine which are the relevant principles), this does not prevent us from saying that some reasons for a given decision are better than others, or that there is a correct answer (even though we may disagree about what it is), or that one party or the other is entitled to a decision in his favor (though, again, we may dispute about which one it is).

The most important questions in connection with legal principles are not whether there are such things or whether their weights are readily determined, but where judges are to get their principles and whether principles are really part of the law at all. After all, might Hart not maintain one or the other of the following: (1) that there are rules *and* other standards (including principles) in a legal system, and that both are ascertainable by means of a social rule of recognition, or (2) that these principles and other standards are not part of the law at all, but are rather extralegal standards that judges may, in the exercise of their discretion, appeal to in deciding hard cases? Either of these alternatives would allow Hart to hold on to the view that law consists of a set of standards (in the first case rules and principles and perhaps other standards, in the second case rules alone), all of which can be identified by the criteria provided by the rule of recognition.

Dworkin's contention is that neither of these moves is open to Hart, and that legal positivism—in particular, Hart's version of it—must be rejected. Against (1) Dworkin argues as follows. Unfortunately for Hart, it is not possible to identify legal principles by their pedigrees—i.e. by content-neutral characteristics that a rule of recognition could specify. Legal principles are not created in acts of legislation, whether legislative or judicial. What characteristics could they have, then, by which they could be identified? Sometimes they are referred to in judicial decisions, and sometimes in preambles to statutes; sometimes they have no explicit statements at all but are inferred from statutes, judicial decisions, or the Constitution. But sometimes the principles are derived directly from morality or from political theory, and not from the foregoing strictly legal materials. None of this permits the formulation of a rule that could be used to identify appropriate legal principles in a content-neutral way. And it will not do to think of the rule of recognition as saying simply that those principles are law that are accepted in the community. Such a move would accomplish nothing, for it would turn out that in effect principles, like the rule of recognition itself, are valid (or legally binding, or something similar) because accepted, and not because they satisfy the test of the rule of recognition.[18] That is, they would have legal effect even without the rule of recognition.

Against (2) Dworkin maintains that the principles in question are *legal* principles, that they are part of the law, and that they must, legally speaking, be taken into account by judges. Judges have a legal duty to recognize certain principles; they can have such a duty only if these principles are legally binding on them; hence these principles are legally binding—i.e. are part of the law. Indeed, Dworkin argues that "unless at least some principles are acknowledged to be binding upon judges, requiring them to reach particular decisions, then no rules, or very few rules, can be said to be binding upon them either."[19] The argument he gives is this: if there are no standards determining when a legal rule may properly be altered or rejected, then all rules are liable (and legitimately, as far as the law is concerned) to judicial alteration or rejection. But not all rules of law are legitimately liable to such alteration or rejection. Thus, "there are standards, themselves binding upon judges, that determine when a judge may overrule or alter an established rule, and when he may not."[20] To regard a particular rule as binding, then, is to regard it as "affirmatively supported by principles the court is not free to disregard, and which are collectively more weighty than other principles that argue for a change."[*]

Dworkin's own view of these matters is grounded in his account

[*] Ronald Dworkin, "The Model of Rules," *University of Chicago Law Review*, 35 (1967): 39. Dworkin points out that among the principles supporting a rule are those of legislative supremacy and precedent.

of judicial discretion and judicial duty. As we have seen, Dworkin distinguishes three senses of the term discretion. In one sense, to say that an official must use discretion in applying a standard is to say that since the standard cannot be applied mechanically, the official must use judgment in applying it—for example, when the sergeant is directed to choose his five most experienced men. In another sense, to say that an official has discretion is to say that he has the final authority with respect to some decision, that his decision cannot be reviewed by another official. This is a sense in which a referee who calls a foul in a game has discretion. Both of these kinds of discretion are present in the law; judges, for example, must exercise judgment in applying standards, and sometimes legal officials have the final authority to make certain determinations. But in both of these cases the official is operating within a framework in which he is applying standards that are given to him by a higher authority, and is not permitted to select the standards that he prefers or thinks appropriate. It is for this reason that Dworkin calls these senses of discretion weak senses, as distinguished from the strong sense in which the official "is simply not bound by standards set by the authority in question."[21] This kind of discretion is called into play, for example, when the sergeant is directed to pick any five men for a patrol, for the directive does not purport to guide his decision, and so he must himself select the standards that he is to use in making his decision.

As Dworkin sees it, Hart is committed to the view that judges have discretion in this strong sense. That is, Hart's view must be that sometimes, when a judge cannot find any applicable or at any rate clearly applicable rule to use in determining the outcome of a case, he must fashion a new rule. Presumably judges do this by appealing to standards that are more general than legal rules, such as general principles. But which principles they appeal to cannot be determined by the rule of recognition, and hence must, on Hart's account, be extralegal standards. Since the appropriate authority (in this case, the body of law itself) does not provide a directive that purports to guide the judge's decision, the judge thus has discretion in the strong sense.

Dworkin rejects this view as incompatible with some important data—namely, that the principles to which judges appeal do control their decisions, that judges must legally (and not just morally) appeal to these principles, that they in fact take themselves to be legally bound by these principles,[22] and that a party in such a case is legally (and not just morally) entitled to a decision in accordance with the weight of the applicable principles.[23]

At this point we again touch base with legal realism—in particular, with some of the realists' arguments we examined earlier. Rather than repeat those arguments and the replies to them, we might merely take note of Dworkin's rejection of the realists' position with regard to these data:

> We make claims of legal right and duty, even when we know these are not demonstrable, and we support these with arguments even when we know that these arguments will not appeal to everyone. We make these arguments . . . to courts. . . . In so doing we assume that some arguments for a given position are better than others, and that the case on one side of a doubtful proposition may be stronger than the case on the other, which is what I take a claim of law in a doubtful case to mean. We distinguish, without too much difficulty, between these arguments and predictions of what the courts will decide. These practices are poorly represented by the theory that judgments of law on doubtful issues are nonsense, or are merely predictions of what the courts will do.[24]

To repeat, Dworkin contends that a judge does not have discretion in the strong sense—that is, discretion to appeal to extralegal standards of his own preference, selected "according to his own lights."[25] Rather, a judge has a duty to appeal to principles, and to appeal to certain principles and not to others, on the appropriate occasions (and he has such a duty even though it is a matter of judgment, and hence involves discretion in one of the weak senses, which principles are the proper ones to appeal to, and also what weights are properly to be assigned to them). Hart's theory, Dworkin argues, does not account for this aspect of official duty.

But then what does account for this judicial duty? Clearly it must be a directive of some sort. But, Dworkin insists, it cannot be a social directive, for the fact is that judges disagree not only about the weights to be given to principles, but about which principles are to be appealed to, and perhaps sometimes even about whether any principles at all are to be appealed to.* But if there is disagreement about what a directive says, it cannot be a social directive, for since social directives are determined entirely by the behavior of the appropriate community, there cannot be a directive where there is disagreement in that community on what is to be done. Hence the directives that constitute or stand behind the duty of judges to apply certain principles and not just any principles they favor—i.e. that make it the case that certain principles are part of the law and hence legally binding—must be normative standards. Dworkin's view, then, as I understand it, is that legal principles are normative and not social in character. They are genuine moral and/or political principles that judges are duty-bound to take into account in reaching their decisions. Though unwritten, these principles are nevertheless part of the law—for as we have seen, the duty that judges have to apply them is a legal and not just a moral duty. Hence the conclusion that the law consists not merely of rules, but of principles (1) that are legally binding on judges, (2) that cannot be identified by a social rule, and (3) whose bindingness on judges cannot be a matter of their being social directives or at least backed up by social directives. Principles of this nature must therefore be viewed as binding moral or political principles that impose legal duties on judges. Only in this way, Dworkin believes, are we able to account for the data.

HOW JUDGES CAN HAVE DUTIES: A POSITIVISTIC REJOINDER

There is, I think, a central premise of Dworkin's argument that underlies a good bit of what he says; and it is important to bring this out clearly, for it seems to me to be mistaken. Dworkin says:

The law does not simply state what private citizens ought or ought not to do; it provides what they have a duty to do or no right to do. It does

---

* I have in mind the question of whether the First Amendment to the Constitution is to be regarded as a rule that may not be outweighed or as a principle that may. See Laurent B. Frantz, "The First Amendment in the Balance," *Yale Law Journal*, 71 (1962); and Charles Fried, "Two Concepts of Interests: Some Reflections on the Supreme Court's Balancing Test," *Harvard Law Review*, 76 (1963).

not, moreover, simply advise judges and other officials about the decisions they ought to reach; it provides that they have a duty to recognize and enforce certain standards. . . . But it is a formidable problem for legal theory to explain why judges have such a duty. Suppose, for example, that a statute provides that in the event of intestacy a man's property descends to his next of kin. Lawyers will say that a judge has a duty to order property distributed in accordance with that statute. But what imposes that duty on the judge? We may want to say that judges are "bound" by a general rule to the effect that they must do what the legislature says, but it is unclear where that rule comes from. We cannot say that the legislature is itself the source of the rule that judges must do what the legislature says, because that explanation presupposes the rule we are trying to justify. Perhaps we can discover a basic legal document, like a constitution, that says either explicitly or implicitly that the judges must follow the legislature. But what imposes a duty on judges to follow the constitution? We cannot say the constitution imposes that duty without begging the question in the same way.[26]

The problem, according to Dworkin, is to explain why judges have duties to do certain things. It cannot be because of a constitution, for example, for though a constitution does specify certain things that judges are to do, it cannot explain their duty to follow it, and hence cannot itself be the source of a judge's duty to comply with it. Positivists (or Hart, at any rate) try to explain the source of judicial duty in terms of a social rule, but this attempt fails, according to Dworkin, largely because no social rule can indicate all of the standards—particularly the principles—that apply. That is, a social rule is unable to tell us what it is that a judge has a duty to do.

What emerges from the foregoing is that there are two problems: to account for all of the duties that judges have, including their duty to apply certain principles; and to account for judges having any duties at all. Dworkin's central premise is that one and the same thing must account for both of these: one and the same directive must answer both the question of how it is that there is any duty at all imposed on a judge, and the question of what that duty is. Moral and political principles—genuinely normative and not merely social ones—are seen as serving this dual function, and so Dworkin argues that such principles must be regarded as part of the legal system. It seems to me, however, that one can have a normative system without agreeing that one and the same item must do both of these jobs. In what follows I shall develop a model of a simple normative system in which this is not the case. The question will then be whether a legal system is sufficiently like the model for us to avoid Dworkin's argument for his view of the role of moral and political principles in a legal system.

In games like cards and football there are certain things that the players must do or avoid doing. Because we do not (usually) talk about duties in these contexts, we will say that requirements are imposed on them. And we will say further that these requirements are imposed by directives, where this is a generic term incorporating standards, principles, rules, policies, and so forth. But now a distinction is needed between a directive's applying to a person (and saying what he is to do), and its imposing a requirement on a person. The need for this distinction can be shown as follows. Suppose in a game of cards we have a rule saying that when situation *s* occurs, the youngest person in the room (even if not a player) must pay a forfeit. Our rule could say this; but though it applies to that person who is the youngest person in the room, even if he is not a player, it does not succeed in imposing a requirement on him, for the obvious reason that he is not playing the game. That is, the rule by itself cannot determine who is a player, and as such required to adhere to it; even its saying he is a player does not make him one.*

What we have said thus far is that a directive does not succeed in imposing a requirement on a person merely by applying to him. Instead a directive that applies to a person imposes a requirement on him only if he is a player, where a player is defined other than as a person to whom a directive applies. And further, being a player is sufficient for a directive that applies to a person to impose a requirement on him. What kind of account can be given of being

---

* Hart makes a related point against Kelsen's contention that a law is valid simply because there is a norm that authorizes the creation of that law or in some other way confers validity on it. See his "Kelsen's Doctrine of the Unity of Law," in Howard E. Kiefer and Milton K. Munitz, eds., *Ethics and Social Justice* (Albany, N.Y., 1968), pp. 178–80, 194.

a player in a game? Hart explains this in terms of social practices and the internal point of view: If a group of people (which may even be a mere collection of individuals who have no previously existing ties) evidences certain behavioral regularities, together with pressure for conformity, criticism of deviance, and so forth, then that group has social rules and the internal point of view; and if a given member of the group takes the internal point of view with respect to these rules, then he is a player. Now this is a sufficient condition for being a player, but it is not clear whether it is also a necessary condition. In a card game we are probably inclined to say that taking the internal point of view—toward most of the rules anyway—is necessary for being a player. But this is not so obvious in the case of a legal system, and Hart has not satisfactorily explained exactly how a person who does not take the internal point of view toward at least certain important rules of a legal system can have any requirements imposed on him. Whereas with respect to our card game we can quite simply say that anyone who ceases to take the internal point of view ceases to be a player, so that the rules of the game no longer impose any requirements on him, this move hardly seems available with respect to the law, since most of the people to whom its rules apply cannot cease to be players. But the difficulty that arises here is not Hart's alone, for it is the central problem of political philosophy to explain how it is that the law succeeds in imposing requirements on certain non-players—or, more accurately, makes players out of those who would not be players.

However crucial this question is when it comes to the law, it seems not to present a similar difficulty for card games. So we can safely develop the model for such a game, and return later to the question of whether the model is instructive in the case of the law.

Suppose our game has officials. How are we to account for there being requirements imposed on them? That is, there are certain directives in our game that have to do with certain specific tasks (official tasks). These standards might apply to non-players, but as before they would not succeed in imposing requirements on them. They impose requirements only if one is in the game, and being in the game is explained as it was before—by one's taking the internal point of view toward the rules (or most of the rules) or toward the game as a whole. So it seems relatively easy to explain how it is that officials in our game have requirements (or in this case we could appropriately say duties) imposed on them; they are in the game in the same way that anyone who is playing cards is in the game.

What we have arrived at here is that in our game of cards we must make the same sort of distinction with respect to officials as we made with respect to ordinary players—that is, between a directive's applying to the official, telling him what to do, and a directive's imposing on an official the requirement to act in accordance with the directives that apply to him, whatever they turn out to be. When it comes to officials in a legal system, however, Dworkin, as we have seen, insists on something different. He insists that the directives that apply to an official of a legal system also account for his having a duty (i.e. for there being a requirement imposed on him) to act in accordance with them. He insists on this, as we have seen, because the directives that apply to a judge might not always tell the judge what to do. And where this is the situation, Dworkin seems to think, there are no requirements at all imposed on the judge in deciding the case—that is, as far as that decision is concerned, the judge is not a player.

Let us see whether this is, or needs to be, the situation in our card game. What we need to do is make our game more complex by giving our officials more to do. Let us consider three cases.

Case A. Suppose an official is authorized to deal with problem cases (e.g. vague rules, new circumstances) by supplying new rules that are fair and that promote the good of the game. What the official is to do is thus specified by the directive that applies to him; but his having a duty (his having a requirement imposed on him) is due not to the fact that the rule applies to him, but rather to the fact that he is a player. One might ask whether this directive really supplies any standard or principle to be appealed to by the official in fashioning new rules, or whether instead it merely authorizes him to appeal to outside standards. There is no apparent reason why we should not take it as doing the former. The principles contained in the directive can certainly help to determine what is to be done, for if an official were, say, to fail to take into consideration the fact that a proposed new rule would unfairly result in certain players always winning (for example, the player who moves first), then he would not be adhering to the directive. Notice, too, that the standards supplied in the directive are moral standards, which via the directive have become part of (have been given a role in) the game.

Case B. Suppose instead an official is authorized to make new rules, but is given no standards to use in performing this task; the pertinent rule merely says something like "The official may supply new rules when necessary" or "The official is to supply the best rules he can think of," and makes no reference to fairness or the like. Here the directive does not provide standards, and the official must provide his own standards for the appraisal of alternative rules. There is only a moral requirement imposed on him to select certain standards (such as fairness and promoting the good of the game) rather than others, and other players have only a moral right to his doing that. However, by virtue of the authorization, the rules selected become rules of the game.

Though the difference between this case and Case A does not seem so great, the disparity in the authorizations could be important. If an official is directed to make new rules that solve problems in the fairest way (and no reference is made, say, to promoting the good of the game), then in a game such as football fan appeal would not be a relevant consideration. But if the directive indicated no standards, and the official had to select standards himself entirely on moral grounds, then the good of the game might well be a relevant consideration. There is also another way in which it can make a difference whether the rule-making authority of officials is governed by specified or unspecified moral standards, for the rules might provide for sanctions against or for removal from office of an official who does not comply with the requirements imposed on him.

Case C. Suppose there is no authorization at all for anyone to provide new rules for the game. Then some problems that arise will be left wholly unprovided for. Now suppose someone takes it on himself to select or propose or provide new rules. This person, like the official in Case B, has only a moral duty to select certain standards, and the other players have only a moral right to his doing so. However, whereas in Case B the rules selected became rules of the game because the official was authorized to make them, in this case they become rules of the game only if they are accepted. And further, if it becomes accepted practice for the player who took it on himself to provide new rules to do so whenever the need arises, then that too becomes a new rule of the game. In similar fashion the principles used in selecting new rules can become part of the game.

Can the person who takes it on himself to provide new rules be regarded as a player in so far as he is engaged in a task that is not authorized, and that involves the selection of rules in the absence of standards provided by the game? No doubt this person is a player to the extent that the existing rules of the game impose requirements on him (though these requirements do not bear on his present undertaking). It is also true that the rules he is selecting are rules for the game; and so we might say that the game thus does impose something on him in connection with his present undertaking, even though no particular directives of the game do; the game might at least be seen as imposing some limitations on his rule-making activity. Or better, we might try to argue that the point or end of the game gets some hold on him; we might then be able to maintain that the game does supply some standards that must be taken into account by anyone who is engaged in making rules for the game. This move might have some force with respect to our card game, but it is not clear whether it can successfully be advanced in the case of the law; this will be taken up in the next chapter.

Let us summarize the points that have been made thus far. The card game of our model is a normative system. The central distinction we used to explain certain features of this normative system is between a directive that merely applies to a person, and one that also imposes requirements on the person to whom it applies. This distinction applies to officials as well as to ordinary players. A directive can authorize an official to make new rules and can specify the standards to be applied. These standards may be moral standards; but if they are, (1) the directive makes these moral standards part of the game, so that an official who applies them is not appealing to extra-systemic standards, and (2) it is not because they are moral standards, but because the official is a player, that he is subject to a requirement (that is, a requirement of the game) to make use of them. However, if the game does not specify such standards or even authorize rule-making, it may be that there is only an extra-systemic moral requirement imposed on the official—though whether this is the case with respect to law has yet to be investigated.

What we have, then, is an account of a kind of normative system in terms of (1) directives that say what is to be done, and by whom, and (2) an explanation of how a person comes to have a requirement imposed on him when a directive applies to him—that is, a way of distinguishing those on whom *any* of the directives of the normative system impose requirements, from those who have *no* requirements imposed on them by the system (even though some of the directives might apply to them). The kind of normative system that we have given an account of is a conventional system—one in which (as characterized by Dworkin) the fact that there is a widespread agreement is an essential part of a person's ground for holding that certain directives impose requirements on himself and others.[27]

Could a legal system be a conventional normative system of the sort described? First of all, on such a view of a legal system we can explain how officials, particularly judges, come to have requirements imposed on them: it is a matter of their being players. Since they are players, whatever legal directives apply to them and tell them what they are to do impose legal requirements (legal duties) on them. And this is the case even for directives, if there are any, that tell judges to appeal to moral principles on certain occasions; the question of a judge's moral duty aside, the existence of a legal directive that directs him to appeal to a moral standard imposes a *legal* requirement on him to appeal to that standard. We need not refer to the moral character of the standard in order to explain a judge's having a requirement imposed on him to apply that standard.

Are there, then, any legal directives that tell judges to appeal to moral principles in certain cases? And, if so, are these directives sufficiently broad to supply all of the principles that are properly regarded as legal principles? Or must judges sometimes appeal to standards that cannot properly be regarded as legal principles? The problem being raised here is whether a legal system (and in particular our legal system) is more like Case A or Case B of our card game. (To the suggestion that it is in some respects analogous to Case C, I would reply that in authorizing judges to decide cases, legal systems authorize them to interpret vague rules and to supply rules where they are lacking, though with respect to the supplying of rules there could be a directive to the contrary.)

A legal system could be like Case A: there could be a directive telling judges to deal with problem cases by appealing to moral standards (or perhaps to the moral standards prevailing in the community, or to moral standards implicit in the legal system, or something of the sort); and this would do the job of ensuring that the law supplied standards for all cases and thus imposed a legal duty on the judge in these cases. Do legal systems contain such directives? More specifically, does our legal system contain such a directive? I would say yes, there probably is such a directive in our own legal system whose existence is evidenced by judicial practice and even judicial pronouncement in opinions and elsewhere. Probably such a directive exists in the same way in many legal systems. But it also seems to me, as I will argue in the next chapter, that such a directive is implicit in the concept of a legal system.

So far, then, a theory of a legal system as a conventional normative system can deal with there being requirements imposed on judges (one side of the problem of judicial duty) and with what judges are to do (that is, with the extent to which the law prescribes official activity, which is the other side of the problem of judicial duty). What of Hart's view that whatever is law has a pedigree—i.e. can be ascertained to be part of the law by a content-neutral (in particular, a morally neutral) test? Three points seem appropriate here. First, a legal principle could be identified by such a test, if, say, the legislature were to require that the judiciary appeal to it. And the criterion for identifying legal directives might be broadened so as to identify as law standards accepted by the judiciary.[28] But (second) since there may be legal principles that have not yet been explicitly formulated or appealed to, then even if an explicit legal directive were to make all moral principles legal principles, it would be quite misleading to insist that as-yet-un-formulated legal principles can be identified by some content-neutral test. Nevertheless (third), the notion of a content-neutral test is not without some use even if it is limited in its application to rules, and not principles, of law. We can simply recast the thesis that there is a social rule of recognition that identifies the law thusly: in every legal system there is a social rule of recognition that identifies the rules of the legal system, and that, if it does not directly identify, at least points the way to, the principles of the legal system.

5

Natural Law

The point we have reached thus far is this. A legal system embodies not only rules of various sorts, but also many principles. All the rules in the system can be identified by their pedigree—by their satisfying certain formal tests specified by the rule of recognition for that system. But the legal principles cannot always be identified in this way. They are part of the system, but they do not always become part of it in the way that the rules do. What else, then, might make them part of the legal system? What is the theoretical underpinning for them?[1]

An age-old view about law called the natural law view would, if true, provide the theoretical underpinning for these principles. Actually, there is no one view that is *the* natural law view. Rather there are many positions that fit this description, especially in ethics. But these many positions, though they can and often do differ in significant ways, all have a central theme, namely, that at least some non-conventional directives for human behavior can be found. Some thinkers have believed that these directives could be discovered by reason. Thus, for example, Thomas Hobbes argued that certain laws of nature could be derived from certain features of human beings and their condition. Such a view is also found among certain contemporary moral philosophers who represent what is called the "good-reasons approach" in ethics.

In its more classical appearances, however, the natural law view holds that there are certain laws operative in nature, and that they can be discovered by intuition or reason or both working together. These laws not only describe the workings of nature, as the laws of physics do, but also prescribe the proper behavior of beings having the capacity to think and to act on the basis of thought. The difference between humans and non-humans in their relation to law is merely that whereas non-humans and inanimate objects cannot violate the laws of nature, human being can and sometimes do. Among the Greeks, for example, such views were connected with a teleological conception of nature, in which each thing, human as well as non-human, is thought to proceed toward a state that constitutes its specific good, the proper end for a thing of that kind. The end or good or perfection of an acorn, for example, is a full grown and healthy oak tree, and in proceeding toward that end, the acorn is behaving as it should. Similarly, on such a view of the world, human beings are thought to have proper ends given by nature, and the only difference between humans and acorns in this respect is that humans may pursue their proper end consciously. What is the proper end or good of human beings? It is a state not only of physical maturity, but of the development of mental excellence and excellence of character (virtues). This is a person's natural end, and anyone who fails to act so as to bring it about is acting contrary to nature, and so should act otherwise.

A non-secular version of natural law is given by Thomas Aquinas. God, on his view, has a plan (the eternal law) for the universe, part of which is constituted by the laws for non-rational things and part for rational beings. Of the laws for rational beings, part (divine law) cannot be discovered by reason and must be revealed, but the rest (natural law) is accessible to human reason. Human intuition reveals the first principle for determining proper human behavior—namely, "that good is to be done and promoted, and evil is to be avoided."[2] Natural laws are supposed to be derivable from this; for example, from this it follows, according to Aquinas, that one should not murder or be cruel.

Natural law theorists have held that there is a connection between natural law and human law (which is the fourth kind of law distinguished by Aquinas). The connection is that if something is a genuine human law it will not violate the natural law. That is, however much something might appear to be law (that is, positive law, or human law), it is not law at all if it violates natural law. This point is sometimes put by saying that an unjust law is no law at all. Or to express it in more modern terminology: being in conformity with correct moral principles is one of the criteria for the validity of law, for being part of a legal system. This picture of human law has been appealing, at least in part, because it explains why there is an obligation to obey the law. It is widely held that there is something about the law that obligates people, and this obligation is thought to be a moral and not merely a legal obligation. Natural law theory explains why there is such an obligation: it is because everything that really is law is in accordance with morality. Since everyone certainly has an obligation to act in accordance with morality, everyone has an obligation to obey the law. And of course all law *is* in accordance with morality, on this view, because being in accordance with morality is one of the criteria for being law at all.

The question with which this chapter began was how we can account for the principles that are part of a legal system. Natural law theory can provide an underpinning for such principles. These principles have to do with justice and fairness and other aspects of morality; for example, "The courts generally refuse to lend themselves to the enforcement of a 'bargain' in which one party has unjustly taken advantage of the economic necessities of another."[3] From a natural law perspective it is evident why such principles are part of the law. These principles could be viewed as part of, or as implied by, the natural law, and thus as providing standards to be used by judges in deciding what the law is and thus what people's legal obligations are. Indeed, a full-blooded natural law theorist might go further and say that no so-called law that is in conflict with these principles is really law at all.

Critics have found much to object to in natural law theory. The Thomistic form of natural law theory has been held to suffer from epistemological difficulties. It holds that the first principle of practical reason is a self-evident truth that we apprehend by intuition.

However, different people's intuitions seem to reveal different and sometimes conflicting things to them, so intuitive apprehension is no guarantee of truth. And even if it is demonstrably a necessary truth "that good is to be done and promoted, and evil is to be avoided," there is the problem of whether this is really the first principle of morality, or merely one among many, for sometimes we appear to have obligations to do things that do not, on these occasions, promote the good—such as keep promises.* Further, even if we were to accept Aquinas's first principle, it is no easy matter to draw conclusions from it. For example, it may be obvious that promoting the good and avoiding evil means not murdering people, but is killing in self-defense permitted by the principle, or is it murder all the same?

The Greek form of natural law theory has been held to have difficulties also. It requires that there be natural purposes or ends or goals, the embodiment or realization of which constitutes the good of the things that have those ends. To explain the behavior of something is thus to show not only how it actually behaves, but also how it should behave. There is a certain plausibility to this in the case of something like a tree, or rather the process of development by which a seed becomes a tree. But it is not so plausible to say that inanimate things like stones have proper ends or specific goods. And in the case of human beings, though it might be plausible to say that survival is a proper end of human activity, with the implication that people ought to behave in certain ways, it is considerably less plausible to say that humans have some specific good that indicates, apart from questions of survival and health, the kinds of lives they ought to lead.

But the most important critique of natural law theories, for our purposes, has to do with the connection between natural law and human law. The natural law view, we saw, is that human law must comply with natural law, and that whatever does not comply with natural law is not law. This position is denied by a great many

---

* Some moral philosophers would agree, however, to a principle like Aquinas's as the first principle of morality if it is interpreted as applying not directly to individual acts, but rather to kinds or classes of acts or to rules for behavior that are to be adopted.

writers on law, and this denial constitutes the basis of legal positivism (in the broad sense in which legal positivism includes, in its analytic aspects, legal realism). What the law is, the positivists say, and what it ought to be are two distinct questions that must not be confused with one another. What the law ought to be, they acknowledge, is an important question, and in fact of the first importance for our lives. But it is the wrong question to ask from the standpoint of legal theory. The aim of legal theory is to give a theory of the law as it is; the data for such a theory are laws as they are found in existing legal systems. A legal theory must identify the criteria for something's being law, and it is the position of the positivists that such criteria are never moral ones. Something may be bad law; it perhaps ought to be otherwise; but if it satisfies certain non-moral criteria, then, however bad, it is law. If the question of whether or not something really is law depended on whether it passed certain moral tests, people would often be in doubt about what the law is, and thus about what is legitimately to be expected of them by others. Such confusion can be avoided only by keeping quite separate the problem of validity (the problem of what the rules of the system are) and the problem of evaluation (what the rules should be).

It is important, however, to be clear about how far the positivists want to extend this separation of law and morality, as it is called. For positivists do not deny that there are some connections between law and morality; they do not deny that a good bit of morality is reflected in law, and they do not deny that there are moral standards appropriate for the appraisal of law. Nor is it incompatible with positivism that the law sometimes, often rightly, requires moral evaluations—as when a statute makes good moral character a condition of naturalization, or when a court refuses to enforce a contract because it is immoral (e.g., is grossly unfair to one of the contractors). And some positivists agree with H. L. A. Hart that extralegal moral standards may be appropriate in statutory or constitutional interpretation. But however close the connections between law and morality, the central point of the positivists is that something can be law even though it fails to satisfy any moral tests: there are no moral criteria for the validity of law (or if there are, there need not be); there are no *logical* connections between law and morals.

Hart, we might note, even concedes that there is a "core of good sense in the doctrine of Natural Law," and argues for what he calls a "simple version of Natural Law."[4] Though it is not logically necessary for law (or morality, for that matter) to have a certain content, according to Hart, there are compelling reasons for it to do so. These reasons have to do with certain "natural facts and aims" of "beings constituted as men are," and these facts and aims form a setting in which a certain content of law is a "natural necessity." The natural facts are that human beings are vulnerable to bodily attack; that they are approximately equal in strength, agility, and intelligence, so that there can be no natural domination, and cooperation becomes necessary; that human beings are neither predominantly selfish nor predominantly altruistic, but rather a bit of each; that resources are limited (making the institution of property necessary); and that human beings have limited understanding and strength of will (making sanctions necessary). The natural aims are minimal: the desire for survival and the desire for social life. Given these natural facts and aims, according to Hart, the law (as well as morality) must have a certain content. But the necessity of this content is natural and not logical; it has only to do with there being good reasons for law and morals to have this content, and nothing at all to do with what the law *is* in any legal system. If the necessity were logical, then anything that was properly called law would, as a matter of logical necessity, have to be compatible with what Hart calls the minimal content of law; but, according to Hart, the connection is not logical, and a valid directive that is incompatible with this content is nevertheless law.

A MODERN NATURAL LAW VIEW

In recent years there has been a resurgence of natural law thinking, connected largely with the writings of Lon L. Fuller. Since Fuller's attempts to argue against the separation of law and morals are, I believe, unconvincing, I will not go into them in great detail. It is worthwhile, though, to see what sorts of arguments he uses, for I think that some of them hint at more satisfactory arguments.

In his book *The Morality of Law* Fuller maintains that the purpose of a legal system is to subject human conduct to the governance of rules. Law, he says, is not merely "there"; it is not a datum to be studied as if it were just another natural fact. Rather, it is an activity, and more specifically, an activity that is the "product of a sustained purposive effort."[5] A legal system must not only be created, but also be maintained, and eight conditions are necessary, he tells us, if a system of legal rules is to be created and maintained: (1) there must be rules; (2) the rules must be publicized; (3) retroactive legislation must not be used abusively; (4) the rules must be understandable; (5) the rules must not be contradictory; (6) the rules must not require conduct beyond the power of the affected parties; (7) the rules must not be changed so frequently that the subject cannot guide his actions by them; and (8) there must be congruence between the rules as announced and their actual administration. A ruler who tried to subject human conduct to the governance of rules but failed to fulfill these conditions would fail in his purpose; hence, the fulfillment of these conditions is necessary.[6]

These conditions constitute what Fuller calls the internal morality of law. The internal morality of law is contrasted with the external morality of law in that the eight conditions are not concerned with any specific topics of lawmaking, such as polygamy, the study of Marx, the worship of God, the progressive income tax, or the subjugation of women. The eight conditions thus form a "procedural" version of natural law—procedural because nothing has been said about the content of the rules of law, and a version of natural law because

a total failure in any one of these eight directions does not simply result in a bad system of law; it results in something that is not properly called a legal system at all, except perhaps in the Pickwickian sense in which a void contract can still be said to be one kind of contract. Certainly there can be no rational ground for asserting that a man can have a moral obligation to obey a legal rule that [fails to meet one of the eight conditions].[7]

The idea here is that if a ruler tries to create a legal system and fails to meet the eight conditions (or even one of them, Fuller maintains), then it is not just that he has created a bad legal system, but that he has created none at all.

Now where in all of this is there supposed to be a connection between law and morality, apart from Fuller's assertion that his eight conditions constitute a morality of law? Perhaps he is correct in saying that a failure of all or even one of the conditions results not merely in a bad legal system but in none at all. But what is the reason for saying, in such circumstances, that there is no legal system because of a failure to accord with morality? For Fuller's eight conditions, being procedural, or content-neutral, seem to be compatible with great evil and injustice; laws can, for example, be applied justly while being substantively unjust. Fuller claims that this is impossible if the eight conditions are satisfied. He maintains that in Nazi Germany, where there were iniquitous laws, most of the eight conditions were violated, and that therefore there was no law at all in Nazi Germany. But this is no argument, for he does not show that the eight conditions *cannot* be satisfied if there is substantive immorality. So Fuller has a natural law position, and an extremely weak one at that, only if the eight conditions are themselves moral requirements. But they hardly look like moral requirements. They are indeed requirements that must on the whole be satisfied if there is to be law. And it is true that some sort of evaluation is required in determining whether they are satisfied; but not all evaluation is moral evaluation. There are standards for writing books and building houses,[8] and failure to comply with them may result in failure to produce a book or a house, but these standards are not moral standards, and failure to comply with them need not be a moral failing. There is thus no justification for calling Fuller's eight conditions moral requirements that must be satisfied if there is to be law at all.

Yet for all this, it may be that Fuller (or one of his partisans) means to maintain that the eight conditions are after all moral principles and not merely strategic principles or the principles of a craft.[9] Suppose, for example, a magistrate were to punish someone for the violation of a vague or inconsistent law. This would surely be unjust; does it not demonstrate that the principle that laws are to be clear and consistent is a moral principle? Now it is certainly true that this magistrate's behavior is unjust; but this does not mean the principle in question is a moral one, for we would surely not want to say that every time a legislature passes a vague or inconsistent law it has done something in the least immoral. Careless, perhaps, and troublesome, but hardly immoral. So the principles in question are not moral principles. The wrongness of the magistrate's act derives not from the violation of that principle of Fuller's, but from the violation of some other, genuinely moral principle.

In an earlier article, entitled "Human Purposes and Natural Law," Fuller attempted to give a different argument for a logical connection between law and morals.[10] In that article, as elsewhere, Fuller sees positivists as insisting on a sharp distinction between the law as it is and the law as it ought to be, and more generally, between "is" statements and "ought" statements, between facts and norms (or in his terms, a distinction between facts and values). This distinction, Fuller believes, is mistaken with regard to law, for law is a purposive activity, and where purposes are involved, according to him, fact and value "merge." Critics of Fuller have pointed out that neither his position nor his arguments are as clear as they should be, and so it is left to his readers to determine just what his theses and arguments are. By my reading of Fuller here, he is saying that the distinction between fact and value is undercut where purposes are involved because purposive behavior cannot be fully understood unless values are brought in. For purposes provide a tool for evaluating the behavior or activity in question, so that what *is* being done and what *ought* to be done come together. Law is a purposive activity, Fuller tells us; hence, in law, is and ought merge.

Now whether law is a purposive activity needs to be shown, and indeed an explanation must be given of what it means to say that an institution or practice has a purpose or purposes. (As we have seen, in *The Morality of Law* Fuller says that *the* purpose of law is to subject human conduct to the governance of rules. We might question whether law has only one purpose, and also whether, if there are many purposes, this is even one of them. It seems to be more like a means for achieving purposes than a purpose itself.) But even if law is indeed a purposive activity, has the merger of fact and value been accomplished? We must determine first exactly what Fuller's thesis is. If it is that there is no tenable distinction at all between fact and value (or norm), Fuller is mistaken. The distinction is clear enough in paradigm cases (contrast, e.g., "Jones has five dollars in his pocket" with "Jones ought to pay Smith five dollars"); and the existence of vague or borderline cases does not show that there is no distinction. Furthermore, there must be some wholly non-evaluative way of identifying the things that are to be evaluated in order to be able to make value judgments about them at all. It may be, however, that Fuller is not claiming that there is no distinction at all, but means only that where there are purposes, the very nature of the thing in question indicates what the proper standards of evaluation are. This is correct; if the purpose of a law is to prevent monopolization of an industry, then we immediately know, at least in part, how to determine whether that law is a good one or a bad one. But likewise if an architect's purpose is to design a building suitable for listening to concerts, we then have some of the standards appropriate for evaluating the goodness or badness of his design. But just as in this case the evaluation in question is not moral evaluation, so also in the case of the law to forestall monopolies. Thus, even if law is a purposive activity, there is not yet sufficient ground for saying that we have found a logical connection between law and morals.

A FUNCTIONAL ACCOUNT OF LAW

I propose now to argue for a natural law view that is not unlike Fuller's attempt to connect morality and law through the notion that the law is a purposive activity. The discussion is divided into three stages, as follows: a discussion of the logic of functional terms and an argument that the concept of a legal system is to be understood functionally (Stage A); an attempt to show that the function (or purpose) of a legal system is in part moral (Stage B); and the assertion that once the function of a legal system has been shown to be in part moral, a connection of the appropriate sort between law and morality is established (Stage C).

Stage A: The Concept of a Legal System as a Functional Concept

We can distinguish in our vocabulary both functional words and non-functional words. "A word is a functional word," says R. M. Hare, "if, in order to explain its meaning fully, we have to say what the object referred to is *for*, or what it is supposed to do."[11] Tools are paradigms of things that have functions; and so are the individuals who use tools professionally. We do not know what a carpenter is, for example, until we know what a carpenter is supposed to do; hence, the word carpenter is a functional word (or, we might say instead, the concept or notion of a carpenter is a functional concept or notion). Or consider a tool like the wrench. A wrench is an instrument of a characteristic shape. But knowing this is not enough for us to know what a wrench is; one must also know that it is used for turning nuts and bolts. (The shape, to be sure, is usually sufficient for identifying a wrench; but being able to identify wrenches is not all there is to knowing what a wrench is.) On the other hand, knowing that wrenches are used for turning nuts and bolts is likewise not enough for us to know what a wrench is; otherwise, anything that had that function (such as a pair of pliers) would be a wrench.

A functional term, then, is understood in part in terms of certain features by which things referred to by that word can be identified and in part in terms of their function. Now in knowing what the function of a thing is, one immediately knows something about the criteria to be used in evaluating that thing, for determining whether it is a good one or a poor one. Thus, since wrenches are used for turning nuts and bolts, it follows that a wrench that cannot be used for turning nuts and bolts—particularly tight ones—is a poor (or at least a defective) wrench, that being able to turn nuts and bolts is a necessary condition for being a good wrench. This evaluative criterion is given to us by the very meaning of the word wrench, or by the concept of a wrench, if we prefer to put it that way.

The function that is part of the concept of a wrench also gives us a way of distinguishing a wrench—a "real" wrench, as we would say in this context—from something that only looks like a wrench. A thing that looks like a wrench but is made of tin foil is not a wrench, not even a poor one, and the reason for this is that it is not even minimally suitable for turning nuts and bolts. But we must be careful here. We do not want to say that anything that cannot be used for turning nuts and bolts is not a wrench, for a wrench that is damaged or has a defect in it that prevents its being used to turn nuts and bolts is nevertheless a wrench. That is, we cannot make it part of the definition of a wrench that whatever is a wrench works. Thus we should say that a thing that has a certain set of physical characteristics (those of a wrench), but is not suitable for turning nuts and bolts and would not be suitable for this even if non-defective, is not a wrench. The functional character of a wrench thus enables us to recognize some poor wrenches (those that, though non-defective, cannot be used for turning nuts and bolts), and it enables us to distinguish some non-wrenches from wrenches (only some, since the non-functional part of the concept of a wrench enables us to distinguish between other non-wrenches and wrenches).[12]

There are two more things to be clear about at this point. We have said that the concept of a wrench provides us with criteria for evaluating wrenches. But knowing what a wrench is does not supply us with all of the criteria for the goodness of wrenches; it permits us to identify some (but not all) of the poor ones. Second, it is obvious that the criteria for the evaluation of wrenches contained in the concept of a wrench do not produce any moral evaluations; they permit us only to distinguish between some wrenches that are good specimens of their kind and others that are not good specimens of their kind. That such criteria are contained in the concept of a wrench does not tell us that wrenches ought, morally, to exist, or that anyone would be morally remiss if he failed to make a good wrench.

Not all terms, as I said at the start, are functional terms. (I will henceforth understand the notion of function in the following way: a concept is functional if, and only if, criteria for evaluating the thing in question are part of the concept; and a thing has a function if, and only if, evaluative criteria are part of the concept of that thing.) The word sunset is not a functional term. Whatever the criteria for the goodness of sunsets are, they are not to be found in the concept of a sunset.[13]

What of the concept of law? Is it a functional concept? Hart and other positivists treat it as a non-functional concept. As Hart sees it, there is no law (other than the rule of recognition) that is not identifiable by means of a content-neutral test, and there are no evaluative criteria that go into the identification of the law. There are, of course, standards for the evaluation of law, according to Hart, but these derive not from the concept of law itself, but (in part) from certain natural necessities. Fuller, on the other hand, treats the concept of law as a functional concept, and thinks that he has found therein an important connection between law and morality. However, as we have seen, not only is his case for taking the concept of law to be functional a weak one, but the evaluative criteria he claims to find implicit in the concept are not, contrary to what he thinks, moral ones.

The law must, logically, have some content or other; it must deal with some matters or other. There are two possibilities I can think of for what something that is called a legal system could be dealing with. The most obvious is the resolution or at least the regulation of conflict, and the other is the expanding of possibilities for what people can do or bring about, the usual examples being laws that enable people to make wills, enter into marriages, and others—activities that could not exist without there being rules that in part constitute those practices and activities, just as the game of baseball could not exist without the rules that constitute it. These two possibilities are not unrelated, however, for if there are laws of the second kind, they themselves create new areas of potential conflict. We are thus, left, I think, with the resolution or at least the regulation of conflict as something that the law must, logically, deal with.

Insofar as there is an end or goal of a legal system, something that it must aim at, and insofar as whatever can be pursued as an end can be done in better or worse ways, we can conclude that the concept of a legal system is a functional concept. But not just any way of doing a better job of resolving or regulating conflicts will be of interest to us. Fuller suggests several ways of doing a better job of this (though he thinks the aim is merely to subject human conduct to the governance of rules, whereas we have seen that a legal system governs conduct by rules in order to achieve certain broadly characterized ends). However, as I have pointed out, Fuller's canons of better lawmaking do not yield the connection between law and morality that he sought. So we want to distinguish better and worse ways of resolving or regulating conflicts, and we want thereby to locate an interesting connection between law and morality. But we must be careful, for conflicts can be resolved or regulated in many different ways, some of them quite undesirable. Indeed, it is apparent that a law that deals with any given subject matter can deal with it in any number of ways without ceasing to be about that subject matter. So we must not beg any questions by picking out evaluative criteria that cannot be defended without appeal to favored political principles.

Stage B: The Moral Function of a Legal System

I suggest that doing a better job of resolving or regulating conflicts that arise among people is in part a matter of doing it with less friction and resistance on the part of those individuals. By friction and resistance I do not mean rebellion or even refusal to comply, though these would be sufficient for saying that the rules were not doing an effective job of dealing with conflict. Agitation, opposition, foot-dragging, malingering, and even persistent grumbling are also kinds or signs of friction and resistance. Even these might be absent, though, if a regime were repressive enough; but this would produce only the appearance that a good job was being done of dealing with conflicts—squashing complaints is not dealing with the problems. So, of two ways of dealing with conflicts, the better way is whichever produces less friction and resistance and would do so if people were free to express themselves. This amounts to saying, I think, that the law achieves this end well only if its rules are such that the addressees of the rules (or as many of them as possible) can accept the rules—i.e. take an internal point of view toward them. We can accordingly ascribe the following function to a legal system, viz., to regulate the conduct of the individuals to whom the rules of the system apply in such a way that most of the rules of the system, and indeed the system itself, can be accepted by those individuals.

Hart sees matters somewhat differently. He maintains that a legal system exists when, and only when, two conditions are satisfied: the valid rules of the system are generally obeyed, and the system's "rules of recognition specifying the criteria of legal validity and its rules of change and adjudication [are] effectively accepted as common public standards of official behaviour by its officials."[14] The officials must take the internal point of view toward the rules for official behavior, but the ordinary individuals need only obey: they may take the external point of view toward the rules that apply to them.

In an extreme case the internal point of view with its characteristic normative use of legal language ("This is a valid rule") might be confined to the official world. . . . [O]nly officials might accept and use the system's criteria of legal validity. The society in which this was so might be deplorably sheeplike; the sheep might end in the slaughterhouse. But there is little reason for thinking that it could not exist or for denying it the title of a legal system.[15]

I do not think that we can go along with this last claim of Hart's. Such a legal system is, on Hart's view, as full-blooded an instance of a legal system as any other. But it seems to me that the situation Hart describes involves something that is at best a limiting case of a legal system, and perhaps ought not to be counted a legal system at all.

Imagine visiting a country of this sort as a guest of its officials, i.e. a country where the system is accepted by the officials but the ordinary individuals take the external point of view toward it. The officials show us how their government and their courts work, and extol their legal system. Note that what we are describing here is not just a dictatorship or oligarchy or something like that, for these sorts of polities are compatible with the ordinary individuals having an internal point of view. What we need to imagine instead is a society run like a concentration camp or a slave labor camp. All of the ordinary individuals, we are to imagine, are put to work, from before dawn until after dark, building, cultivating, or whatever, not for the benefit of themselves or of future generations of ordinary individuals, but solely for the benefit of the officials. Here are some sample rules governing the ordinary individuals in this society: anyone who looks at an official is punished; anyone who fails to fulfill his work quota does not eat; anyone who has in his possession anything but his clothing is punished; anyone who takes the rations of another is put to death. We can imagine more rules of the same sort. We can also imagine that in the courts alleged infractions are tried with the utmost seriousness, that every reasonable attempt is made to distinguish the guilty from the innocent, and even that excuses (mistake, accident, etc.) are recognized.

The question is whether we are prepared to say that these rules and the apparatus for enforcing them are seriously to be taken as constituting a legal system, or whether they instead constitute a parody of law—all form and no substance. The use that is sometimes made of the concept of democracy provides us with an apt comparison. Many countries call themselves democracies on the ground that they go through ritualistic elections every so often; but usually we know that this is just a sham, and that these countries are not democracies at all. I am suggesting that just as these countries cannot properly be called democracies, the system of governance we have described above has only the trappings of a legal system, and is not properly speaking a legal system at all. And I think this is so even if certain minimal requirements of administering a system of rules are met—in particular, even if the eight conditions that Fuller calls the internal morality of law are fulfilled.

We must be clear about one thing before going on. The claim advanced here is not that there are no rules existing in this imagined society. Nothing that Hart says concerning the existence and identification of rules has been questioned. There are purely formal tests for determining what the rules are. What has been questioned is whether Hart is correct in saying that a system of rules that satisfy such tests is in all cases a *legal* system. The claim I am making instead is that among systems of rules some may be legal systems and others not, and that the system described above is not a legal system.

If it is not a legal system, why not? What is missing? What is missing is that this system of rules is not one toward which the ordinary individuals can take an internal point of view. It is not enough, in order for there to be a legal system, that only the officials take an internal point of view toward the rules and others in the society merely obey them. It is also necessary that the ordinary individuals, or at least most of them, regard the system itself from the internal point of view. Thus, in order for a system of rules to be a legal system, it must be such that it can be accepted by most of the ordinary individuals. We might say, aphoristically, that the possibility of a legal system is just the possibility of the internal point of view being taken by the ordinary individuals.

This claim, centering as it does on people's attitude toward a system as a whole, is a significant departure from Hart's views, for according to him one takes an internal or external point of view toward individual laws.* Hart is partially mistaken here, I believe, and the effect of the mistake is to obscure the real character of a legal system. Take as an example a law requiring the filing of

* Most people, says Alexander Bickel, "are, in truth, in a state of assent, acquiescence or relative indifference toward each law, and in a state of acceptance of the notion of a legal order and of the legitimacy of this one" ("Civil Disobedience and the Duty to Obey," *Gonzaga Law Review,* 8 [1973]: 205).

income tax returns. It seems to me that a person can have an internal point of view toward this law only if he has a certain attitude toward the legal system as a whole. How can a person take this law as a standard for how he and others ought to behave if he does not, among other things, view the imposition of taxes as a legitimate thing for a government to do and also view the people who levy it as entitled to do so? Thus, to have an internal point of view toward at least certain laws logically requires that one have an internal point of view toward other laws and toward the system as a whole. The acceptance of certain laws requires the acceptance of the system of which they are a part. This is not the case for the external point of view, however; taking the external point of view toward particular laws is compatible with taking either the internal or the external point of view toward the system as a whole.

All this suggests that whereas the concept of a legal system is functional, the notion of a law should not be understood in exactly the same way. For one thing, the one is not fully understandable without the other: we cannot understand what a law is if we do not know what a legal system is; laws must be seen as belonging to legal systems. It might be helpful for some purposes (though it is also misleading in some ways) to say that whereas the concept of a legal system is functional the concept of a law is not; rather, the concept of a law is the concept of a rule (or an explicitly recognized directive of another kind) that is part of a system of a certain sort, and it is its belonging to such a system that makes it a law. This helps us to locate the difficulty with a theory of law that, like Hart's, takes the concept of *a* law and the problem of the validity of laws as its central features. The concept of a legal system is more than the concept of a set of rules, each of which satisfies certain formal criteria. But focusing too narrowly on individual rules of law has the effect of obscuring the fact that the two things are not one and the same.

The claim being made, then, is that the function of a legal system is to regulate the conduct of the individuals to whom the rules of the system apply in such a way that the system itself can be accepted by those individuals, and hence that a system of rules is a legal system only if it can be accepted by most of the ordinary individuals to whom it applies. Note that it is not part of the concept of a legal system that the system is actually accepted; people might refuse to accept a system and hence its rules for poor reasons.

Nothing has been said yet about what is meant by the requirement that the system *can be accepted* by the individuals to whom the rules apply. The notion of acceptance, or taking the internal point of view, points the way here. There is more to this than just a person's feelings or emotional response to a rule or a system of rules; it is a matter of a person's having or adopting an attitude, which involves at least in part conscious deliberation and evaluation—i.e. the consideration of reasons.[16] For example, to take an external point of view toward a rule is to be prepared to comply with it, and to think that one should do this because of the adverse consequences of noncompliance. Likewise, to take an internal point of view is to think that one ought to comply because . . . , where an appropriate sort of reason is filled in after the "because." * In short, the internal point of view involves, among other things, having reasons for compliance. Thus, a legal system is defined as (1) a set of directives, including a rule of recognition, (2) which regulates the conduct of ordinary individuals to whom the rules apply in such a way that the system itself can rationally be accepted by those individuals.

We must be clear about the sense of "rational" intended here. Sometimes when we say that doing such and such would not be rational (or would be irrational), we mean there is a superior alternative available; and the principle involved is that rationality demands that of two alternatives, the one supported by the better reasons be selected. This is not the principle of rationality intended in our definition of a legal system. The sense of rational in the definition is a minimal sense, according to which it is rational to do only that for which there is some (though perhaps not the best) reason, and irrational to do that which is not at all supported

---

* "Because it is the law" could be a person's reason, provided that he for other reasons takes the internal point of view toward the system as a whole.

by reason. In this sense of rationality a system of rules can rationally be accepted (regarded from the internal point of view) only if there is some reason of the appropriate sort for doing so.

There is a limited number of possible reasons for accepting a legal system. Promoting justice, promoting the good of people (oneself or others), and promoting personal or social ideals seem to exhaust the possibilities. We do not need to pursue the question of which of these are the most appropriate reasons, but two points should be made. First, a person might rationally go along with a legal system and profess adherence to it for purely self-interested reasons. But such a person accepts the legal system in the required sense only if he is willing to hold that there might be occasions on which either he or others ought to comply with the law even though it is against his or their overall self-interest to do so. Otherwise that person has adopted an external point of view toward the system. Second, though I will not argue the point here, it seems clear that if the promotion of justice and the promotion of ideals are to count as reasons, they must be connected in some way with the good of people. In Plato's *Republic* one of the disputants argues that justice is not to be counted a good thing if it is not beneficial. Whatever the connection between justice and human good is, it seems to me that this point is well taken, though the challenge of finding the connection remains.[17] A similar point can be made with regard to ideals.

If now we use the phrase "promote human good" to stand for any of the three sorts of reasons mentioned above, we can draw together several strands of our discussion in this chapter. We can say that if a system of rules cannot promote the good of the people being regulated by them, then it cannot rationally be accepted by these people (unless they are quite mistaken about the effects of these rules). And if a system of rules cannot rationally be accepted, then it fails in its function and is thus not a legal system at all. Our functional characterization of a legal system thus provides us with criteria for distinguishing between systems of rules that are and that are not legal systems; and the same criteria also permit us to distinguish between worse and better legal systems. For if being a legal system at all implies satisfying certain criteria at least to the degree that the system can rationally be accepted, then the more rational it would be to accept it (i.e. the greater the degree to which the criteria are satisfied), the better the legal system is. We can, additionally, go one step further. The criteria that we have found to be implicit in the concept of a legal system can be used to evaluate not only a system of rules, but also particular rules within the system. This is not to say that rules that fail miserably by these criteria are not rules of the system; whether they are or not is determined by the rule of recognition. It is only to say that we can distinguish between better and worse rules of the system. If too many rules fail miserably by the criteria in question, there would be no legal system; but this only shows that the criteria for the existence of a legal system and for the validity of rules within such a system are different.

The criteria that we have found implicit in the concept of a legal system are, quite evidently, moral ones, for they all come roughly under the heading "promoting human good," which is clearly a central demand of morality. No attempt has been made to spell this out in any way. Sometimes it is clear what the requirements of justice and the common good are, and sometimes there is disagreement. But that there may be disagreement about exactly what the criteria implicit in the concept of a legal system are, or about exactly how they are to be applied, does not show that there are no such criteria at all. We may not all agree that something is a good wrench, or even a wrench at all; but this does not mean there are no evaluative criteria implicit in the concept of a wrench. It is the same with the concept of a legal system, and it makes no difference that the criteria are moral ones.

Stage C: The Theory Expanded and Explained

If, as I claim, there are criteria for the evaluation of law implicit in the concept of a legal system, and these criteria are moral ones, then we have found a connection between law and morality of the sort that natural law theorists have sought. Yet there are, I believe, a few independent points that might profitably be pursued to expand and explain what has been developed so far.

First, not all of the criteria by which legal systems may be evaluated are implicit in the concept of a legal system, nor are all of them moral criteria. Legal systems can, for example, be more or less efficient and can cost more or less to operate—a legal system is better if it is more efficient and less costly. Thus, one legal system can be better than another without being morally better, though one can also be better than another by being morally better.

Second, given the account of natural law that has been developed, we are in a position to see that natural law is compatible with positivism. They are compatible as long as none of the criteria for the evaluation of rules of law are made part of the criteria of validity for legal rules and other created legal directives. The natural law position we have set out does not imply that an unjust law is not a law (though a thoroughly unjust system of rules is not a legal system); validity and morality are distinct. Further, natural law is compatible with the notion that a legal system is in part a conventional normative system, for our theory of natural law does not detract from the view that legal rules and other created legal directives impose requirements on individuals and on officials by virtue of the existence of social rules.

Third, it is sometimes said that there is a prima facie moral obligation (not just a legal obligation) to obey the law—i.e. to obey all of the laws. If there is such an obligation, it cannot be because each law is required by or is even in accordance with morality, for some laws are morally indifferent and others may even be morally bad; and yet, I believe, this obligation extends to these laws as it does to others. Those who think there is such an obligation do not agree on what underlies it—though most agree that there must be something besides the mere fact of a law's existence that creates the prima facie obligation to comply with it. What this might be will be discussed in due course, but for now the important thing to consider is that if there is such an obligation, then different features of the concept of a legal system can point the way to *conflicting* prima facie obligations. For if there is an obligation to obey the law, then the fact that some rule *r* satisfies the criteria of validity of a legal system gives rise to a prima facie obligation to comply with *r*; but if *r* at the same time violates the moral criteria implicit in the concept of a legal system, this gives rise (or at least may give rise) to a prima facie obligation *not* to comply with *r*, since *r* ought not to be a part of that legal system. Indeed, in the latter case, a litigant who opposes a law on moral grounds might argue that the law is on his side—meaning by this that, as he sees it, there are legal principles that require the court to change a particular rule of the system.[18]

Finally, let us consider the following, written by R. M. Hare:

> [If] "horse" is used as a functional word, meaning "charger," a horse that throws his rider becomes *eo ipso* a bad one; but the *horse* might say to himself "I'm not trying to be a horse in *that* sense; I'm only a solid-hoofed perissodactyl quadruped (equus caballus), having a flowing mane and tail," and proceed to throw his rider without offence to anything except the rider's standards. For, though the meaning of the word "charger" determines some of the qualities of a good charger, that of the word "horse," in the more general definition given by the *O.E.D.*, does not; in this sense of "horse," the question of what horses ought to do with themselves remains open. Just *because* the horse cannot choose but to be a horse in this general sense, the fact that it is a horse in this general sense does not determine whether or not it ought to choose to be a good charger. It may not regard the choice before it as a choice, what sort of charger to be, but only, more generally, what sort of horse to be. The horsebreaker's art would be easy if one could turn horses into chargers by definition.[19]

This line of thought, when applied to the concept of law, might seem to undercut the natural law view we have developed. The argument would be that if "legal system" is used in a functional sense, then a legal system that fails in ways that have been discussed is indeed a bad legal system. But a system of rules cannot be turned into a legal system (where this is a functional notion) just by calling it one. Just as calling a horse a charger cannot yield the conclusion that it is a bad horse if it does not behave like a charger, so likewise we cannot say that a system of rules is a bad system of rules because it fails to measure up to the criteria for legal systems.

But this argument is beside the point, for our natural law theory does not imply that any system of rules is bad as a system of rules if it does not behave like a legal system. What it implies is that certain possible systems of rules are not legal systems even if some people call them legal systems.

Perhaps Hare's argument is intended to make a different point. We have the concept of a charger, and this concept has certain evaluative criteria built into it, but this does not mean that we ought to try to train horses to be chargers, or that horses ought to try to be chargers. There are no implications for what anyone ought to do that follow from the fact that the concept of a charger is a functional concept. So likewise one might argue that the fact that the concept of a legal system is functional does not imply that we ought to create legal systems, or that we are doing anything wrong if we create systems of rules that are not legal systems. It is true that *if* we want to create a legal system we must satisfy certain criteria, just as if we want to have chargers we must satisfy certain criteria; but if we do not want to do these things, those criteria have no hold on us, they impose no unconditional requirements.

Why should this point be thought to be damaging for our account of a legal system? It could be taken to be damaging, I believe, only if one were to see the claim of a necessary connection between law and morality as meaning that the mere fact that evaluative criteria are implicit in the concept of a legal system implies that certain behavior is unconditionally required of us, and particularly of those who make and administer the rules. But if it is indeed true that certain behavior is unconditionally required of us, this is not because the concept of a legal system is a functional concept, but because the standards implicit in the concept are, unlike the standards implicit in the concept of a charger, moral ones.

Many moral philosophers take very seriously the question "Why be moral?," though they find it difficult to answer. We will not take up this question here, beyond noting that it is a significant one—and that the question "Why have law?" is in large part the same question. Once we have decided to have a system of governance by rules, the question arises of whether the system shall

satisfy moral criteria and thus be a legal system—that is, whether
we should be moral in this aspect of our lives. No analysis of the
concept of a legal system can answer this question for us, but this
does not mean that there are no moral criteria implicit in the concept of a legal system, or that there is nothing important about
saying there are such criteria.

Having completed this tour of legal theory, we return to the
question raised at the outset of this chapter—namely, what is
the theoretical underpinning for the principles that we find in a
legal system, since their place in a legal system cannot always be
explained by the notion of validity? These principles constitute
or are implied by the moral criteria that are implicit in the concept of a legal system. They are part of the legal system even
though the notion of validity does not always apply to them, and
they are, in a sense, there all the time. Certain moral requirements
do get explicitly formulated in judicial decisions, and the doctrine
of precedent may apply to such formulations, as well as to rules.
But explicit formulation is not required in order for the moral criteria that are implicit in the concept of a legal system to be part
of a legal system.

Some of the principles are fairly narrow and relatively easy to
apply; others are quite broad and accordingly not easy to apply.
Further, principles often conflict with one another in their application in particular cases. Though these features of principles often
make it difficult to determine what the proper outcome of a case is,
this difficulty is only to be expected where people have different
beliefs about what morality requires; and even if there were uniformity in such beliefs, it would be difficult to be sure what the
right answers are. We must not think, though, that because people
do not agree on what the moral criteria are that are implicit in
the concept of a legal system, or on what principles are implied
by these criteria, or on how particular cases should come out, this
shows that our view is mistaken. The difficulty of determining
what the correct answers are in moral matters often tempts people

to try to escape such questions altogether; but these questions are really inescapable, and such temptations are to be resisted.

A few final points. First, we can see, given the underpinning that we have found for principles, why it is they have the logical features they have—that is, why they do not set out legal consequences that follow automatically when the conditions provided are met, and why they have the dimension of weight or importance. The explanation is that they embody moral precepts, which can come into conflict, which can be broad or narrow, and which can be more or less weighty, morally speaking. Second, we might note that these principles play three roles: (1) they are used in the criticism of rules of law—for a rule that contravenes one of these principles is still a rule, and indeed the fact that a rule contravenes a principle does not mean that it should not be a rule of the system, for there may be better reasons in terms of the principles to have it than to get rid of it; (2) principles have a role in judicial decision-making when it is not clear what the rules require in a particular case; and (3) principles sometimes have a role in alleviating the consequences of the application of a rule where such application would work an unjustice or a hardship on some people —the granting of equitable relief.

Finally, realists are impressed by the creative or inventive task in judicial decision-making. There is more to judicial decision-making, they say, than the mechanical application of rules. They are surely right about this. But I have argued that where rules do not clearly apply, and sometimes even where they do clearly apply, there are principles within a legal system that are the correct ones to appeal to, and these principles determine what result should be reached. This point is not undermined by the fact that principles have different weights that are unquantifiable, for the notion of a correct result still applies.[20] But if this is so, then do judges not in fact discover the law rather than make it? Is not judicial decision-making a mechanical procedure after all? What place is there for the exercise of the judicial virtues that we most admire, the ones that are connected with what is called judicial lawmaking? The answer to these questions is clear enough. The virtues of inventiveness and creativity are quite compatible with the notion of discovery, the notion that there are correct results to be found. To say there are criteria for correct lawmaking is not to take away the creative task in lawmaking any more than in physics. The difference lies in the degree of certainty we can attain that a given result is the correct one, or that we have found results that we should hold on to.

6

Law and Obligation

Law is binding on those to whom it applies. This bindingness is often expressed by saying that law imposes obligations on people. But what is an obligation? And how does the law create obligations? Are there peculiarly legal obligations, as distinct from moral obligations, and are there other sorts of obligations as well? If so, what is the connection between legal and moral obligation, and between each of these and other sorts of obligation?

John Austin gives the following account of obligation. He says that *"command, duty,* and *sanction* are inseparably connected terms. ... Each of the three terms *signifies* the same notion: but each *denotes* a different part of that notion, and *connotes* the residue." The term command, he says, denotes "the expression or intimation of the wish"; "sanction" denotes the evil to be visited for noncompliance. He then says: "When I am talking *directly* of the chance of incurring the evil, or (changing the expression) of the liability or obnoxiousness to the evil, I employ the term *duty,* or the term *obligation*: The liability or obnoxiousness to the evil being put foremost, and the rest of the complex notion being signified implicitly."[1]

Richard Taylor has put forward a similar view in his 1968 article, "Law and Morality":

The concept of *legal* obligation is entirely exhausted by, and definable in terms of, enforceability. To say that one is legally obligated to perform or refrain, in accordance with a command—e.g., to pay support to a former spouse more wealthy than himself, or damages for injuries for which he was in no way at fault—is simply to say that pains, penalties, and forfeitures can be imposed upon him for failure to comply.[2]

This view of obligation has the untoward consequence that a person has no legal obligation where there is no prospect of his being caught and punished. A person whose earnings are undetectable would have no obligation to make a full declaration of them on his tax return, a person who had escaped the jurisdiction would have no obligation to register for the draft, and a public official might have no obligation to enforce the laws. These consequences seem mistaken.

The Austin-Taylor view of obligation is not very plausible. As we saw earlier, there is a decided difference between being obliged to hand over money at a gunman's demand and being obligated to pay money under a tax law. True, the gunman's threat reduces our options, and so does the law; both require us to turn over some money; to this extent they are alike. But in the gunman situation we have no duty to give up our money; we are merely forced into it at the point of a gun. Austin and Taylor have perhaps given us an account (or part of an account) of being obliged, but not of being obligated.* Whatever the proper account of the binding character of law turns out to be, it must show the law to be binding irrespective of the prospects of incurring a sanction.

H. L. A. Hart has a more sophisticated, though related, account of obligation:

To understand the general idea of obligation as a necessary preliminary to understanding it in its legal form, we must turn to a different social situation which, unlike the gunman situation, includes the existence of social rules; for this situation contributes to the meaning of the statement that a person has an obligation in two ways. First, the existence of such rules, making certain types of behaviour a standard, is the normal, though unstated, background or proper context for such a statement; and secondly, the distinctive function of such a statement is to apply such a rule to a particular person by calling attention to the fact that his case falls under it.[3]

---

* One may perhaps be obliged, though, *by* being obligated: the obligation may make other alternatives unreasonable.

To ascribe an obligation to a person is, Hart says, to point out that his situation falls under a social rule. However, not all social rules impose obligations, according to Hart. The social rules that do impose obligations are those that (1) are thought to be important so that there is social insistence on conformity, (2) are thought important because they are "believed necessary to the maintenance of social life," and (3) are those "characteristically involving sacrifice and renunciation."[4] Legal rules exhibit these characteristics, and thus are obligation-imposing rules. Hart does not deny that there is a connection between obligation and sanction, but he sees it as an indirect connection. Unless sanctions (physical sanctions for the most part) were usually imposed on offenders, "there would be little or no point in making particular statements about a person's obligations"; thus, statements about people's legal obligations presuppose "the continued normal operation of the system of sanctions."[5] This connection between obligation and sanction is only indirect, however, because in individual cases there can be an obligation even if there is little or no prospect of incurring a sanction.

Hart's view that there are certain obligation-imposing social rules, and that a person is under an obligation when one of these rules applies to him is certainly plausible. But do such rules really impose obligations? These rules exist, as Hart sees it, because people take the internal point of view toward them. Those who take this point of view may be obligated because they have imposed the obligation on themselves. If I, for example, adopt a principle as a standard for the behavior of myself and others, I thereby think that they *and I* ought to behave in a certain way. Hence one might say that having adopted the principle, I am obligated to act in accordance with it. But how does my, or many people's, adopting (accepting) it obligate those who do not accept it? On the one hand we do not, I think, want to say that if many people accept an invidiously discriminatory rule, for example, those who do not accept it are nevertheless obligated to comply with it; or at the very least we should not say that they are obligated merely because others have accepted the rule. On the other hand, it will not do to say simply that those who do not accept a rule have no obligation to comply with it, for that could lead to the type of situation Kurt Baier has described:

Suppose Smith and Jones are aliens. The law under which they live requires aliens to notify the police of any change of address within a week. Both have moved recently. Then Jones who "accepts" the law has an obligation to report the change, but Smith who does not "accept" that law, but merely wishes to keep out of trouble, does not have an obligation to report.[6]

REQUIREMENTS AND OBLIGATIONS

Let us step back for a moment and try to get a clearer picture of what we are looking for. The problem is to say something about legal bindingness, and this something, according to Austin and others, is more than simply that various rules of law apply to us, impose requirements on us, give us directives, or whatever. The bindingness of law, they say, is a matter of obligation: the legal requirements that apply to us are thought either to be or to give rise to obligations. However, it is not moral obligation that arises, or at least not immediately. That is, what legal requirements give rise to in the first instance are peculiarly legal obligations, which are distinct from moral obligations. Thus, for example, though there is no difficulty in understanding how an order (or demand) backed by a threat binds a person, Austin goes on to say that such orders create obligations, though not moral obligations. And though we understand, from Hart's explanation, how social rules exist and apply to us, he likewise goes on to say that such rules create obligations, though not moral obligations.

But perhaps we can suggest that this peculiarly legal obligation is just so much extra baggage. If legal obligations were obligations in the same sense of the word in which moral obligations are obligations, and yet were not instances of moral obligation, then when legal and moral obligations came into conflict in a particular case we could imagine the legal obligation taking precedence over the moral obligation. But since a judgment of moral obligation is an all-inclusive judgment (rather than a prima facie judgment), legal obligation cannot take precedence over it. Therefore, either legal obligations are also moral obligations, or legal and moral obligations cannot be obligations in the same sense. The first, if correct, rules out the notion that there is such a thing as a distinctive legal obligation. If it is not correct, then we are left to solve the mystery of what sort of obligation it is that is involved in legal obligation; one suspects that it is merely a matter of there being a legal directive that applies to a person. Of course, people do use the expression legal obligation, but what they always seem to be talking about is either the requirements that various valid rules of law impose on us or else the moral obligations that arise out of these legal requirements. For my own part, I prefer to dispense with the term altogether; I think that by referring only to valid legal requirements, on the one hand, and to prima facie moral obligation on the other, we can express all that needs to be expressed. This usage seems to me to make the most sense, considering first, that there are so-called legal obligations when, and only when, there are legal requirements imposed on individuals; and second, that when a legal requirement is imposed, the only remaining question of any interest is whether one ought (morally) to comply with it.

There are requirements imposed on us in areas other than the law. Requirements are imposed on us in sports and games (e.g. in chess to remove a check on one's king if possible); our economic institutions direct businessmen to act in certain ways (e.g. to compete rather than cooperate in many areas); social institutions require that people behave in certain ways (e.g. to remove one's hat in church); and there are non-institutionalized social rules that apply to us, such as rules of etiquette and correct speech. Legal requirements, such as that citizens pay taxes and pay damages to those they negligently injure, or that officials enforce the laws, are similar to these in the sense that all of them impose requirements on us, and in all cases the existence of these requirements does not in itself provide an answer to the question of whether we are obligated (morally) to comply with them.

Put in the most general way, then, the question at this point is how we can get from the requirements imposed by games, practices, social rules, and institutions to what we ought, morally speaking, to do. More particularly, it is a matter of bridging the gap between requirements imposed by legal institutions and prima facie moral obligation. Some philosophers have thought that for some institutional requirements, at least, there is a logical connection, or something like a logical connection, between the institutional requirement and what we ought (prima facie) to do. The argument, as presented by John Searle, is as follows: [7]

> (1) Jones uttered the words "I hereby promise to pay you, Smith, five dollars."
> (2) Jones promised to pay Smith five dollars.
> (3) Jones placed himself under (undertook) an obligation to pay Smith five dollars.
> (4) Jones is under an obligation to pay Smith five dollars.
> (5) Jones ought to pay Smith five dollars.

Searle's claim is that the first statement is clearly a matter of observable fact, and that each subsequent statement follows logically from the preceding one. Thus, he says, a way has been found to connect, at least in the case of promises, institutional requirements with claims about what we ought, non-institutionally, to do.

No one (to my knowledge) has claimed to have a similar argument connecting legal requirements with what we ought, non-institutionally, to do, so it is not clear what implications this has for law. But in any event the success of the argument even in the case of promissory obligation is doubtful. For one thing, it is doubtful whether all utterances such as those in the first premise give rise even to the institutional requirement that they be fulfilled, and, second, even if such a requirement is indeed created, it is not always the case that one ought (prima facie) to act in accordance with that requirement. Consider the following. Within the institution of slavery a person can make another his slave by performing certain acts; call those acts x. Then:

> (1⋆) Jones did x to S.
> (2⋆) S is Jones's slave.

(3★) S has come under an obligation not to escape.

(4★) S is under an obligation not to escape.

(5★) S ought not to escape (or: As regards his obligation
      not to escape, S ought not to escape).

This argument is exactly parallel to Searle's. "Slave" gets its meaning from the constitutive rules of the institution of slavery, and hence there are suppressed tautological premises that carry the argument from (1★) to (3★). But the argument is invalid, for its conclusion is false. A slave (at least, one who has been taken by capture) has no (non-prudential) reason not to escape; it is not even that there is some reason (his "obligation") that is overridden.*

If this is indeed a counterexample, then "One ought to fulfill one's obligations, other things being equal" is not a tautology, and the question of what one ought, other things being equal, to do is not determined by the meanings of the terms defined by the constitutive rules of institutions. It requires an external (synthetic) principle to get from so-called institutional obligations to oughts. What has misled Searle is the word obligation, which seems to be analytically connected with "ought": it seems to be a contradiction to say "I agree that I have an obligation to do x, but even as regards that obligation it is not true that I ought to do x." But this may not be a contradiction, as we can see by getting clear about what an institutionally imposed obligation is.†

---

* Searle objects to similar examples on the ground that they are based on "an incorrect conception of obligations." "The notion of an obligation is closely tied to the notion of accepting, acknowledging, recognizing, undertaking, etc., obligations in such a way as to render the notion of an obligation essentially a contractual notion" (*Speech Acts*, Cambridge, Eng., 1970, p. 189). But if this is so, then it *a priori* cannot be part of the meaning of "slave" that such a person is under an obligation. But as a matter of fact it is as much a part of the meaning of "slave" that a slave is someone's property and is not to deprive the owner of his property, as it is of "promise" that a promisor is to do what is promised. One who does not understand that slaves are not to escape does not understand what "slave" means. If Searle is right about the meaning of "obligation," then the notion of a slave is self-contradictory, and there logically cannot be slaves. This is surely false. Some aspects of the question of what an obligation is will be considered in the sequel.

† There is, however, an analytic connection between "moral obligation" and "moral ought."

If an institution exists, then there exist certain rules (constitutive of that institution); and some of these rules apply to various people and say what they are to do or refrain from doing. But the mere fact that a rule applies to someone, telling him what to do, does not mean that he ought (other things being equal) to comply with it. Suppose there is a game with a rule saying that whoever enters the room where the game is being played at stage S in the game is the whitser and must pay a forfeit. Then we can construct the following argument, analogous to Searle's:

(1') Jones walked into the room at stage s of the game.
(2') Jones is the whitser.
(3') Jones has come under an obligation to do x.
(4') Jones is under an obligation to do x.
(5') As regards that obligation, Jones ought to do x.

It is clear in this case that a rule applies to Jones and tells him what he is to do. It is equally clear that it is not the case that Jones, who merely walked into the room and thus became the whitser, ought (other things being equal) to pay a forfeit just because of the meaning of "whitser" (which gets its meaning from the constitutive rules of the game). For in the following rewrite of (3')–(5') it is evident that (5'') does not follow:

(3'') Jones has come within a rule requiring him to do x.
(4'') Jones is required by a rule to do x.
(5'') As regards that rule, Jones ought to do x.

The appearance of validity in the original argument is created by the term obligation. We can, if we wish, maintain a tight (analytic) connection between "obligation" and "ought," but then we must explain when being the addressee of a rule imposes an obligation on one, and this cannot be explained, as the foregoing example makes clear, by pointing to a meaning rule. We can, on the other hand, use the word obligation in such a way that a rule such as the one in the example does impose an obligation when it applies to a person, but then we must acknowledge that there is not an analytic connection between "obligation" and "ought."

Thus, to return to Searle's argument, neither the utterance of promissory language nor the creation thereby of a requirement that one act in accordance with that promise *logically* yields the conclusion that one has an obligation (even prima facie) so to act. The only way to get from the making of a promise, or from the existence of an institutional requirement that one act in a promise-keeping way, to the claim that in all cases where the institutional requirement exists one ought (prima facie) to act in that way, is via a moral principle to the effect that one ought to keep one's promises, or at least certain of one's promises. And in general the only way to get from any institutional requirement to what a person ought (prima facie) to do is via a moral principle to the effect that one ought (prima facie) to act in that way. In the case of law the bridge principle is the obligation to obey the law, which is the principle, or part of the principle, of political obligation.

THE OBLIGATION TO OBEY THE LAW

The next question to ask, then, is whether there is such an obligation—whether, that is, "because it is the law" is always *a* reason (a moral reason and not merely a prudential one), independent of the content of a given law, for doing what the law requires. There are indeed many attempts in the political and philosophical literature to show that there is no such obligation,[8] but we will instead look briefly at some attempts to show that there is such an obligation and what its basis is.

Preliminary to this, however, we must be clear on three points. First, the denial that there is such an obligation does not amount to an endorsement of unlawful behavior, for there are many other obligations that might bear on particular cases. All that would be denied is that because something is required by law, this is in itself a reason for doing it. For example, even if there is no special obligation to obey the law, the homicide laws should be obeyed because the prohibited acts are objectionable on other grounds. Indeed, failing any special obligation to obey the law there could even be good moral reasons for obeying some bad laws—for instance, when the consequences of noncompliance would be worse than those of compliance. Second, the reference above to the basis of the obligation to obey the law means that this obligation is not as basic as, say, the obligation not to harm others or the obligation to act justly. The obligation to obey the law needs to be justified or explained by showing how it is backed up by some more basic moral principle. Finally, in thinking about whether there is an obligation to obey the law, it is helpful to keep in mind that if there is such an obligation it might turn out to be in force even when a particular law is bad or unjust. If there is an obligation to obey such a law it might be outweighed (and perhaps even usually is), but the point is that if there is such an obligation it *needs* to be outweighed before one is justified in violating the law. Whether or not there is an obligation to obey the law can thus make a difference to what we should do. We will now look briefly at some attempts to show that there is a prima facie obligation to obey the law, and later inquire whether or not this applies to all laws, however bad or unjust.

One of the oldest and best-known defenses of the obligation to obey the law is the theory of the social contract. The idea here is that each individual is obligated to obey the law because he is a party to a social contract; his commitment derives from his having entered into an agreement. Thus, the basis of the obligation to obey the law is the obligation to keep promises. Some versions of the contract argument maintain in addition that the state, like a voluntary association, is created by these mutual promises, and that in creating the state or government individuals become obligated to obey its rules. This addition to the contract doctrine is perhaps plausible to the extent that the members of the founding generation have, by their voluntary acts, placed themselves under an obligation; but not all states are founded in this way (for some are the result of conquest), and in any event this will not account for the obligation of the descendants of the founders to obey the law. There are, to be sure, certain citizens—naturalized ones—who have explicitly promised to obey the law, but this is not the case with natural-born citizens. In order to apply the classical contract idea to these individuals, resort must be had to the notion of an implicit promise. But this notion seems to be too weak to support a voluntarily undertaken obligation. How, after all, does one make an implicit promise? Is an individual free to refuse to do so? If so, how does he do this? The answers that have been given to these questions constitute what is called the consent theory.

Consent theory is simply a weakened version of contract theory, and hence the obligation to obey the law is again said to be based on the obligation to keep promises. The idea is that acquiescence amounts to consent. If a citizen acquiesces in laws, he is taken to have consented to them, and hence to have undertaken an obligation. Now it is certainly true that acquiescence sometimes amounts to consent. For example, if a military officer sees one of his men do something wrong and fails to order him to stop, he has acquiesced in that behavior and thereby consented to it. It is as if he had given the man permission to do what he is doing. Or if some people are debating a policy, those who do not raise objections can usually be deemed to have acquiesced in it and hence to have consented to it. Is the relation of the citizen to the laws analogous to these cases? What amounts to acquiescence in the laws? Does compliance do it? But compliance may be due only to the fear of sanctions. The appropriate question to ask is what would count as non-acquiescence, for what is notable in the situations described above is that the individuals in question had the opportunity to register their non-acquiescence, and it is clear what acts would count as registering non-acquiescence. Citizens, however, are not in this position; the individual citizen seldom has the opportunity or the means to indicate non-acquiescence either to particular laws or to the system of government as a whole. But absent these, it seems farfetched to say that a person has acquiesced, or at least that he has done so in such a way as to amount to consent.

The preceding defenses of the obligation to obey the law have tried to ground it in voluntary undertakings on the part of the citizenry. The next defense also looks to that ground, but in a different way. It bases the obligation to obey the law on the duty of fair play. This is the principle that where there is a mutually beneficial and just scheme of social cooperation, the success of which requires that all or nearly all cooperate, a person who has accepted the benefits of the scheme and intends to continue doing so is bound by a duty of fair play to do his part when it is his turn and not to take advantage of the situation by not cooperating. Examples of the application of the duty of fair play are cooperative activities such as voting and tax-paying. The idea with regard to law as an institution is that the organization of political society is beneficial to everyone and sometimes requires burdensome acts (obedience to law). No particular act of noncompliance is likely to upset the system or even necessarily have bad consequences, but the duty of fair play entails that citizens who have benefited from the cooperative scheme (in particular, by their fellow citizens' compliance with the law) and intend to continue to do so have an obligation to do what it requires of them when it is their turn. That is, they have an obligation to obey the law.*

Another defense of the obligation to obey the law is the utilitarian approach. The obligation might be said to exist because the existence of a stable legal system has great utility, and acts of compliance promote stability while acts of noncompliance lead to instability. Even if some acts of noncompliance do not weaken the legal system, some utilitarians maintain that the obligation is in force nevertheless; we need not go into this.[9]

A defense advanced by some writers is similar to this, but shifts the emphasis to the individual's benefit from having the institutions of government and law. This might be called the rule egoist view. The idea is that there are certain interests, common to everyone, which can be promoted only through the social cooperation that the existence of political society makes possible. It is thus rational

---

* This argument appears in John Rawls, "Legal Obligation and the Duty of Fair Play," in Sidney Hook, ed., *Law and Philosophy* (New York, 1964). In *A Theory of Justice* (Cambridge, Mass., 1971), Rawls alters his position somewhat. Distinguishing sharply between the notions of obligation and duty, he maintains that the *obligation* to obey the law applies only to officials in connection with the duties of office, but not to citizens generally. Citizens do have, though, a *natural duty* to support just institutions—to "comply with and to do our share in just institutions when they exist and apply to us" (p. 334; see also pp. 113–14). Since compliance is a natural duty rather than an obligation, the citizen need not perform any voluntary act in order to be bound.

for each individual to support the rules and institutions of political society, including such a social device as political authority, or government. But such rules, or at least the weightiest of them, are, it is said, constitutive of morality: morality has to do with what it is reasonable for any individual to do from the standpoint of his enlightened self-interest. Hence, because there are reasons of this sort for complying with law, there is an obligation to obey it.

Finally, the obligation to obey the law is sometimes defended on the ground that law is necessary in order to get people to act in accordance with their moral obligations. In other words, the law and legal institutions secure people's moral rights and promote justice, and there is an obligation to support an institution that is capable of, and perhaps necessary for, promoting such ends in the least undesirable way—provided, of course, that the legal institutions are successful in this.

ULTRA VIRES ENACTMENTS

Having reviewed briefly several attempts to defend the obligation to obey the law, let us assume there is indeed such an obligation—that is, that one of these defenses, or some other, is satisfactory, at least for laws that are not bad or unjust. Wherever the subsequent discussion depends on what the basis of the obligation is, I shall point this out. The question now is whether this obligation applies to all laws, even those that are bad or unjust. But before we address that question, we must first consider the different but sometimes related question of whether a directive is a valid legal directive that really imposes a legal requirement on an individual.

Let us begin by noting that those who make our laws have the authority to do so, and that only the directives created by these individuals count as law. Where these individuals get their authority is, of course, the central question of political philosophy. Austin answers it by denying, in effect, that there is any such thing as the authority to make law. John Chipman Gray holds that authority to make law is conferred by the "real rulers" of society, with respect to whom the notion of authority, as distinct from naked power, does not apply. According to the positivist Hans Kelsen, this authority is conferred by a written or unwritten constitution; and that such a constitution does confer lawmaking authority is taken to be a fundamental postulate, an assumption without which there could be no such thing as valid law. Hart answers the question in terms of the existence of social rules that confer lawmaking authority by creating legal capacities.

Now what is especially important, if we believe there is lawmaking authority, is that this authority comes by way of an *authorization,* and the extent of the authority is determined by what is contained in the authorization. The authority conferred may be completely unlimited: it may be merely a blanket authorization to issue directives dealing in any way with any matter. But it may, on the other hand, be limited in a variety of ways. Our Constitution, for example, authorizes certain individuals to create legal directives, and also imposes limits on the lawmaking authority. Given this, however, we are faced with two problems. First, what are we to say of a directive, created by the authorities of a legal system, that is in violation of their authorization (i.e. is ultra vires)? Is it law or is it not? Is a requirement imposed on us or not? And second, what if the limitations on lawmaking authority, as contained in the authorization, are moral ones? These questions seem to me to bring to the fore some of the basic disagreements between positivists and their detractors. The first question locates a dispute between positivists and realists. According to the realists, what counts as law is what is actually imposed on citizens, particularly by the courts, and if any of this is contrary to an authorization that is written down somewhere, that makes no difference. The law is what the courts are doing, not what some documents say; and positivists, as realists see it, are committed to a contrary position. The second question brings into focus the following problem. If the authorization is construed as imposing moral limitations on lawmaking authority, and if we say that a directive that lawmakers issue contrary to their authorization is at no time a valid law and hence at no time imposes a requirement on citizens, then it looks as if we are saying that there may be moral criteria for the validity of law. This is not exactly the classical natural law position, since the moral limitations are relevant to validity, not because they are the dictates of morality, but only because they have been *made* relevant. Nevertheless, there might be in this a suggestion for a contemporary version of classical natural law theory.

The possibility we are considering, then, is that there is no prima facie obligation to obey a bad or unjust law where there are moral limitations on the authorization of the lawmaking authority, since there is such an obligation only where there is law, and an ultra vires enactment is not law. The question, then, is whether being within the authorization of the officials is one of the criteria of validity for laws.* In order to have a focus for discussion, suppose Congress passed a tax statute that was patently in violation of the Constitution. Would a citizen be legally required to comply with this statute? Let us suppose further that though tax officials have indicated they are going to collect taxes under this statute, the courts have not yet spoken. Is the citizen who refuses to comply violating the law? One line of thought on this question is represented by the judicial opinion in *People* v. *Weintraub*. This case involved several people who had been convicted of violating a statute that was later, and in a different case, declared unconstitutional. The court said:

Holding that a law is unconstitutional is quite different from holding that a defendant has not received constitutional treatment under a law. In the latter case the law is still there. He may be guilty, though certain of his rights may have been overridden. But, if the law is unconstitutional, there is no law and there can be no question about proper procedures for protecting his rights under the law because in theory his

* If criteria of validity are contained in a rule of recognition, which is a social rule, then it is probably vague on this point, and hence there is no rule governing this question. On this, see Ronald Dworkin, "Social Rules and Legal Theory," *Yale Law Journal*, 81 (1972): 863–64. The discussion, then, must concern what the rule of recognition should be. Hart, however, apparently holds that ultra vires acts are not law. See *The Concept of Law* (Oxford, Eng., 1961), p. 69 and *passim*.

rights have never been threatened or affected, and he should be placed in the position he occupied before he was arrested.*

There is another line of thought, however, that we might consider. We might say instead that the statute is the law until it is declared unconstitutional, at which point it ceases to be the law.† The ruling of the court in *Weintraub* could then be interpreted as the judicial creation of a new law to the following effect: when a person is disadvantaged in certain ways (which the court would try to specify) by the application of a law that is found to be unconstitutional, that person is to be placed, so far as possible, in the position he would have been in had the law never existed. Notice, by the way, that an equivalent piece of judicial legislation is needed even on the first line of thought. The court in *People* v. *Weintraub* must be taken as having created a new law to the effect that when a person is disadvantaged by the application of a directive that has mistakenly been taken to be law, that person is to be placed, so far as possible, in the position he would have been in had that invalid directive never existed. For though such treatment certainly is a requirement of justice, it is not a valid directive, to be acted on by officials, until it is made such by someone competent to do so.

---

* 20 Ill. App. 3d 1090, 313 N.E. 2d 606, at 608 (1974). The Weintraub case is to be distinguished from two closely related kinds of cases. The first kind of related case is explained in Cummings v. Morez, 42 Cal. App. 3d 66, 116 Cal. Rptr. 586, at 590 (1974): "It is the general rule that a decision of a court of supreme jurisdiction is retrospective in its operation. . . . A well-recognized exception to this general rule is that, where a constitutional provision or statute has received a given construction by a court of last resort and contracts have been made or property rights acquired under and in accordance with its decision, such contracts will not be invalidated nor will vested rights acquired under the decision be impaired by a change of construction adopted in a subsequent decision." To illustrate the second kind of related case, let us suppose that a special prosecutor prosecutes and gets convictions against certain individuals. The statute creating the office of special prosecutor is later declared unconstitutional, though the laws under which the convictions were obtained are not. Do the acts of the prosecutor until his office is declared unconstitutional have the force of law? The court in State v. Poulin, 105 Me. 224, 74 A. 119, 24 L.R.A., N.S. 408 (1909), answered in the affirmative.

† This line of thought is entertained by Marcus Singer in "Hart's Concept of Law," *Journal of Philosophy*, 60 (1963): 206. This is not to say, however,

It seems to me that the second line of thought, treating the directive as a valid law until declared invalid, is preferable for the following reasons. First, in the usual case the statute in question is not so obviously unconstitutional as our hypothetical tax law. So, though a tax statute so flawed would probably not play the role in the lives of most citizens that valid laws typically play, most unconstitutional statutes do. Having as they do one of the central characteristics of law, as well as the usual "external" characteristics of valid laws, they are best treated as valid laws that do in fact impose requirements on citizens. Second, though a person may be confident that he is correct about the unconstitutionality of a statute, he can seldom be sure that he will prevail. Accordingly, he should take the attitude that sufficiently strong reasons are required for him to be justified in not complying. This amounts, it would appear, to saying that one has as strong a prima facie obligation to comply with such directives as to comply with valid laws, and it provides another good reason for treating such directives as valid laws.

Returning to the extreme case of our hypothetical tax statute, should we say that because it is so obviously outside the authority of the lawmakers, it is not law even though less obviously unconstitutional statutes are valid laws? There does not seem to be much reason to hold this view. Other things being equal, it would be better, because simpler, to treat all unconstitutional statutes alike. And other things do seem to be equal, for no one's behavior should be altered if such a statute is thought to be valid law or the reverse. A conscientious citizen, to be sure, is prepared to obey the law; but a conscientious citizen is not a robot, and only a robot would think that his situation would be different if this particular statute was valid law. Moreover, if the enactment in question has the appearance of being law, then a person who violates it has the appearance of being a scofflaw unless he violates it in such a way as to make it apparent to others that he regards it as invalid. So it would seem

---

that there are not other cases, not having to do with the validity of statutes, in which something (such as a marriage or other contractual arrangement) is void *ab initio* and not merely voidable. See Chapter 7.

that one has as least this much in the way of an obligation with
respect to ultra vires enactments: one must conduct oneself, when
violating such enactments, much as a civil disobedient must conduct himself when violating a valid law. This implies that there is
a prima facie obligation to comply with the ultra vires enactment
because of its having the appearance of law. If there is precisely
the same reason for complying with valid and with ultra vires
enactments, then both should be regarded as law. We could say,
alternatively, that there is a prima facie obligation to obey the law
and, for the same reasons, to obey whatever has the appearance of
law.

There is, admittedly, a recent line of judicial opinions that
appear to express a contrary view. The 1969 case of *Shuttlesworth*
v. *Birmingham* involved a local ordinance requiring a person to
obtain a permit in order to engage in certain activities on public
property. Defendant, knowing he would be refused a permit for
a protest march, did not apply for one, and was arrested for conducting the march without a permit. The Supreme Court over-
turned his conviction, holding that the licensing ordinance was
"unconstitutional on its face," and saying that "a person faced with
. . . an unconstitutional licensing law may ignore it and engage
with impunity in the exercise of the right of free expression [under
the First Amendment] for which the law purports to require a
license."[10] The court thus expresses the view that a law that is
unconstitutional on its face is not valid—is no law at all—and hence
imposes no requirement on an individual.* A closer look, however,
reveals that the passage in question is merely a dictum, and not at
all essential to the result the court wanted to reach. The problem
was this: the court thought that if it said the local ordinance was
valid, then defendant, since he had not attempted to comply with
it, would be barred from raising the question of its constitutionality

---

* But it is worth noting that the Supreme Court does not apply this line
of thought to at least some unconstitutional judicial decrees. Alexander Bickel
reports this as follows: "There was no duty [according to the Supreme Court]
to obey the invalid statute, but there was a duty to obey the invalid court
order issued under it" ("Civil Disobedience and the Duty to Obey," *Gonzaga
Law Review*, 8 [1973]: 212). See Walker v. Birmingham, 388 U.S. 307
(1967).

in his defense. But the court could very well have reached this result directly, without adding the gratuitous remarks about "facially unconstitutional" laws being no laws at all. Indeed, the point had been made twenty-six years earlier by Chief Justice Harlan Stone: "The Constitution can hardly be thought to deny to one subject to the restraints of such an ordinance the right to attack its constitutionality, because he has not yielded to its demands."[11] All things considered, then, the reasons given previously for regarding even "facially unconstitutional" statutes as law seem to have more weight than the reasons to the contrary.

BAD OR UNJUST LAWS

We are now ready to consider the suggestion that the prima facie obligation to obey the law applies to all laws, even bad or unjust ones. There are, however, three other possibilities having to do with bad or unjust laws to consider along with this one. The first is at the other extreme: it is the view that no such directive could be a legal directive. The other two possibilities are midway between these extremes. Both of them require that a distinction be drawn between more and less obnoxious or unjust laws. The first of the middle positions holds that not all attempts to create legal directives are successful; more specifically, even some attempts that are carried out in the prescribed ways (e.g. by enactment, promulgation) are unsuccessful. When a lawmaker acts in these prescribed ways the presumption is that he has created a legal directive, but this presumption may be rebutted. The presumption will be rebutted when the result is extremely and apparently violative of moral standards. Appearances to the contrary notwithstanding, no legally binding directive is created in such cases, and since this is so there is no prima facie moral obligation to comply.[12] The other middle position is similar to this one. It holds that in such cases law is created, and a legal requirement is imposed; and the presumption then is that this legal requirement gives rise to a prima facie moral obligation to comply. But this presumption can and will be rebutted when what the law requires is sufficiently violative of moral standards.[13]

The four positions, then, are:

1. No directive that violates moral standards is a legal directive (imposes a binding legal requirement), no matter how it is created.

2. No directive that is extremely and apparently violative of moral standards is a legal directive, though all other appropriately created directives are.

3. All appropriately created directives are legal directives, but those that are extremely and apparently violative of moral standards do not give rise to a prima facie moral obligation to comply with them.

4. All appropriately created directives are legal directives, and all valid legal directives give rise to a prima facie moral obligation to comply with them.

Much has been said already about the first two positions. Both are forms of classical natural law theory, and throughout this book reasons have been given for maintaining the distinction between what the law is and what it should be (and the related distinction between rules and principles). In the preceding section, reasons were given for holding on to this distinction even when the laws involved are ultra vires.

As between the third and fourth positions, some might be inclined to say that in certain cases there is no obligation at all, rather than that there is an obligation that is overridden. But consider the following argument. Sometimes there is an on-balance obligation to comply with a bad or unjust law (think here of one that is not extremely violative of moral standards); and it seems possible that it is the fact that a law is involved that tips the balance in favor of the obligation. So in such cases, at least, there is a prima facie obligation to obey the law just because it is the law. But if there is sometimes a prima facie obligation to obey the law as such, then there is such an obligation with respect to all laws. Therefore there is in all cases a prima facie obligation to obey the law. It might be objected that in the situation described in the first premise what tips the balance is not that a law is involved, but that other aspects of the situation bring other obligations into play—such as an obligation to avoid disrupting certain social institutions, practices, or other aspects of social order. However (limiting the rebuttal to this suggestion), the only reason that certain acts are disruptive of society is that there are laws involved (the laws constitute, as it were, the order of society that is being disrupted). So in certain cases in which there is surely an obligation, all things considered, to obey a bad law, it would seem that this obligation can be explained only by supposing that there is either a prima facie obligation to obey the law as such or some other obligation that *effectively amounts to* that obligation.

This argument aside, there does not seem to be much to choose between the third and fourth positions, at least with regard to what anyone ever ought to do. For in any situation in which one might be inclined to say (applying 3) that there is not even a prima facie obligation to obey the law, he would also say (applying 4) that if there is a prima facie obligation to obey the law, it is outweighed.[14] In short, it appears that what we ought in the end to do will be the same no matter which position we accept. It is important to bear in mind, though, that the third position is limited to legal directives that are extremely violative of morality—a standard that is not very precise and indeed is disputed. The following passage indicates some of the kinds of cases that one writer takes to rebut the presumption that a valid legal directive ought, prima facie, to be obeyed:

Consider, as possible examples, laws restricting personal behavior that does not affect other people, such as [some] laws about sexual behavior. ... Doubtless many of these are dead letters, but some are not. Or consider the Connecticut law [since declared unconstitutional] forbidding physicians to give birth-control information or the Pennsylvania law (recently declared unconstitutional) requiring teachers to begin the day's work with certain religious exercises. Physicians and teachers might obey these laws from fear of the consequences of infraction, but it seems dubious to say they had a prima facie moral obligation to obey.[15]

Now though we might agree with the author of these remarks that the laws referred to are violative of morality, it does not seem clear that these are the kinds of cases in which "because it is the law" is no reason at all for doing what the directive requires. These seem to be the kinds of cases in which many unquestionably sincere individuals have thought that such laws were not violative of morality, and in which our own commitment to a just constitution and to the legitimacy of most of the institutions and procedures established under it have some hold on us, even if we think that in the end noncompliance is morally justified.

In this connection, most people probably think that before resorting to civil disobedience, a person ought, if possible, to exhaust available legal avenues, though some laws may be so bad that this requirement does not obtain.* The cases we are considering, or others similar to them, such as certain cases of induction into the armed services, seem to me to be cases in which a person would be required, morally, to exhaust his legal avenues before engaging in illegal behavior. But if this is so, then there must be a prima facie obligation to obey the law in such cases, for if there were not it is hard to see why one should first search for legal means of dealing with the situation.

All things considered, the case for the fourth position seems to be the strongest, though I do not see any significant difference between that position and a proper application of the third one. Adopting the fourth position has the virtue of making more visible the important point that in cases in which civil disobedience is being considered there is a prima facie obligation to seek legal means of dealing with the problem.

STRENGTH OF THE OBLIGATION

Some of the foregoing considerations direct us to the question of the strength of the prima facie obligation to obey the law and of what can override it. To show, first of all, that the obligation may

---

* Several Supreme Court decisions have made this distinction. With regard to judicial and administrative orders that are not patently objectionable, a violator will escape punishment only if he has exhausted his available remedies; but if such orders are patently objectionable, he need not exhaust his available remedies. However, with regard to statutes, and also some police orders and arrests, the requirement that one exhaust one's available remedies does not apply: if the violator is declared to be right on the merits of the case, he is not punished. See Mortimer R. Kadish and Sanford H. Kadish, *Discretion to Disobey* (Stanford, Calif., 1973), pp. 100–120.

sometimes be overridden, even with respect to a good law of a just state, consider this case:

In the Commonwealth of Pennsylvania it is unlawful to operate a motor vehicle that has not been inspected. The penalty is not high—perhaps $25, more or less, depending on the whims of the magistrate. But the action *is* unlawful. Now suppose an uninspected car is the only vehicle available for transporting an ill person to a hospital for urgently needed care.[16]

It is of course difficult to state principles that tell us clearly when "because it is the law" is a decisive reason and when it is not. But a few remarks can be made.

Consider first cases in which we are concerned about the harmful consequences of obeying or violating a law. Sometimes, as the automobile inspection case above shows, it is permissible to violate even a good law when obedience would produce bad consequences; here the obligation to obey the law is overridden. If, on the other hand, a person wanted to use an uninspected car to pick up his laundry, the obligation to obey would not be overridden. In general, the less harmful the violative act, the more acceptable a violation having good consequences; but the consequences must themselves be sufficiently good.

Another class of cases involves good laws that are at times both pointless and inconvenient to obey. For example, traffic laws might not permit turns at a red light, but there are occasions when, with a long, clear view in all directions and no oncoming traffic, some people see no moral reason whatever to refrain from making a turn. Now though I agree that it is pointless to wait at a red light in these circumstances, it is not evident to me that there are no relevant moral considerations. But if there is indeed no moral impropriety in violating the law in such a case, I think this can be explained without rejecting the prima facie obligation to obey the law. Obligations can differ in strength: the obligation not to harm others is generally regarded as stronger than the obligation to do good for others. But not only can obligations of different kinds differ in strength, obligations of the same kind can vary in strength as they apply to different sorts of cases. For example, the obligation to keep promises where one takes an oath might be weightier than for promises where one does not, and the obligation to be beneficent might be weightier in the case of humans than in the case of non-humans. The obligation to keep promises and the duty to tell the truth can in some common social contexts have virtually no weight whatsoever, perhaps not even enough to require a person to inconvenience himself. So likewise, perhaps, with the obligation to obey the law. Rather than these last cases being test cases for the existence of the respective obligations, they are at most limiting cases of these obligations.

Sometimes the problem with a law is not that it is a good law that on occasion might have bad consequences, but that the law itself is ill-conceived and its general implementation will have bad consequences. Here we might think of a tax law, or a rationing system, or a price freeze, or a ban on Sunday driving as a fuel-saving measure. Now if what we are concerned about is the general bad consequences of compliance, and not rights or justice, then it does not seem likely that the obligation to obey would be overridden. Indeed, the obligation to obey seems to have its most significant impact with regard to laws embodying political policies of this sort. For if our commitment to certain political procedures and institutions is not reflected here, then it would not seem to be much of a commitment.

More difficult problems are raised when we consider laws that are themselves immoral or unjust or violative of rights, or that have unfair results when applied. Among laws that violate rights, probably the easiest case is that in which a law as promulgated is in direct conflict with an important political right—for example, a law that imposes restraints on mere discussion. Somewhat more difficult is a law that establishes procedures to ensure a right (say, the right to a fair trial), but where the procedures actually threaten the right. More difficult still is a law that is (apparently) aimed at something quite different from our political rights, but that adversely affects some right as an apparently unintended consequence. As to the first of these—a law directly countering an important political right—it seems likely that the obligation to obey is overridden. The second case, involving unjust procedures, seems similar to the first, but it may be more like the third case. It sometimes happens that laws aimed at legitimate ends necessarily infringe on people's rights, though this infringement is not in itself an aim of the law. The constitutionality of these laws is always in doubt, and in recent years there has been controversy over whether such inroads into constitutionally protected rights are permissible; the debate has centered on the question of whether it is acceptable to *balance* constitutional provisions against the legitimate ends of such laws.[17] In such cases the obligation to obey the law seems to have weight, though this does not rule out the possibility of violating such a law so as to test it judicially or to bring its wisdom into question. What makes cases like this difficult is that some laws of this sort may be defensible even though they curtail some rights. It will often be a close question whether such a law is defensible, and there will usually be quite respectable reasons supporting it. Of course the lawmaker may be mistaken. But, again, our adherence to our political procedures must make a difference somewhere, and this too might be an appropriate place—where the competing considerations seem to present a close case, where serious and sincere people who are committed to basic political rights and to the political system differ, and, most important, where the officials charged especially with the task of looking out for these rights have spoken.

The same considerations apply also in other sorts of cases. Where a law appears to violate some moral standard but does not violate an important political right, the strength of the obligation to obey might well be a matter of the extent of the disagreement among serious people over whether the law is violative of morality. It might be that some laws dealing with sexual behavior and drug use fall into this area. Finally, similar considerations apply in the case of laws that either make unfair discriminations among classes of individuals or result in the unfair treatment of certain classes of individuals.

7

Law, Coercion, and Sanction

It is widely held that sanctions, coercion, and force play an important and indeed necessary role in law, and that an understanding of these is essential to a proper understanding of law and legal systems. Among those who have emphasized the connection between law and sanction or coercion are the historical figures Thomas Aquinas, Thomas Hobbes, Immanuel Kant, Jeremy Bentham, and John Austin, and in more modern times, Hans Kelsen, H. L. A. Hart, Jerome Hall, and Joseph Raz. Lately, Hans Oberdiek, in a 1976 article on the subject, has expressed doubts about this connection.[1] In this chapter I will try to provide additional perspectives on the notion of a sanction, and will argue for the necessity of sanctions in the law.

THE NATURE OF SANCTIONS

Nullity and Sanctions

H. L. A. Hart has given what have come to be influential arguments against the view of John Austin and others that nullity is a sanction.[2] Hart gives two arguments for rejecting that view. One runs like this. A sanction can, logically, be detached from a rule prohibiting certain behavior, and the rule will still be intelligible. But nullity cannot likewise be detached and leave an intelligible rule that the threat of nullity supports. This is so because if a law provides a way of doing something, there logically must be a way of failing to do it, and without this latter being a "part" of the rule, there can be no intelligible rule at all—that is, there can be no description of how the thing in question is to be accomplished.

Philip Mullock, considering this argument in his article "Nullity and Sanction" (1974), finds it unsound, and contends that there is after all no logical distinction between nullity and sanction. Mullock distinguishes between the failure to comply with a power-conferring rule and the declaration of nullity based on the failure to comply. This is, he says, formally analogous to the distinction between the violation of a primary rule and the imposition of a sanction based on its violation. Since these are formally analogous, then just as the imposition of a sanction is contingently related to the rule prescribing certain behavior, so also is a declaration of nullity contingently related to the rule prescribing how a given legal act is to be performed. Since the connection between rule and nullity is thus shown to be contingent, the rule is intelligible quite apart from the nullity. Hence, he concludes, Hart has shown no logical difference between nullity and sanction.[3]

Now it is true, as Mullock points out, that some defective wills are probated, but this does not show that such wills are legally null and void only if declared to be so. And though a declaration of nullity is merely a contingent consequence of failure to comply with the rule, its being null and void due to noncompliance is not. The rejection of Mullock's argument thus requires the affirmation of the claim that something (e.g. a contract or a will) can be void though not declared to be so, and hence may be void even though the parties act under its provisions and even though it is officially (but mistakenly) declared to be operative. These consequences of rejecting Mullock's position are quite acceptable; only the acceptance of a realist view of law would, from the standpoint of legal theory, prevent our accepting them. But there is not much to such a view of law; "void only if voided" is too much like "it is illegal only if you get caught."

The law itself supports the view that a contract that is defective in certain ways is void *ab initio* and before being declared to be so.

The law distinguishes between contracts that are void and those that are voidable; Mullock's view would often fail to uphold such a distinction.

A voidable marriage is valid and not *ipso facto* void, until sentence of nullity is obtained. A void marriage is void *ab initio*. The judgment of nullity is merely declaratory that no marriage in law ever existed. . . . Civil disabilities, such as a prior marriage, want of age, idiocy, inability to consent, and the like make the contract of marriage void *ab initio* and not merely voidable. They render the parties incapable of contracting.[4]

Consider the case of *Sutton* v. *Leib*, which involves a woman (plaintiff) who was divorced from defendant in 1939 and awarded alimony for as long as she remained unmarried. In 1944 she married Henzel, but that marriage was later (1947) declared null and void because Henzel had another wife at the time of the marriage. Plaintiff then married for a third time. She brought suit against her first husband for forty installments of back alimony for the period from the date of her second marriage to the date of her third. The court awarded her the back alimony, saying that "a void marriage, as distinguished from a voidable one, is an absolute nullity for all purposes, and no judicial proceedings or decree are required to establish its invalidity."[*] Strange as the facts of this case may seem, they are not unique, and the result is not an anomaly but rather the established rule.[5]

Hart's second argument is that sanctions can be distinguished from nullity because unlike nullity, they are intended to discourage or suppress certain behavior (which behavior is specified by the rule to which the sanction is appended). Hart says:

In the case of a rule of criminal law we can identify and distinguish two things: a certain type of conduct which the rule prohibits, and a sanction intended to discourage it. But how could we consider in this light such desirable social activities as men making each other promises which do not satisfy legal requirements as to form? This is not like the conduct discouraged by the criminal law, something which the legal rules stipu-

[*] 199 F.2d 163, at 164 (7th Cir., 1952). It is worth noting that the court's having previously (but mistakenly) declared the second marriage valid—the decision was overruled by the U.S. Supreme Court—did not affect the outcome.

lating legal forms for contracts are designed to suppress. The rules merely withhold legal recognition from them.[6]

This is perhaps not so much an argument as just an attempt to set things out in such a way that we can see that they are correctly described. However, though the distinction to which Hart draws our attention—between a rule proscribing certain behavior and a sanction designed to discourage noncompliance—is correct, it is not the case that nullity could never fit this model. Suppose a legislature were to pass a law against shopkeepers entering into contracts with minors, but instead of imposing a fine or jail term for violations they think it a sufficient deterrent to say that such contracts are null and void and therefore unenforceable in courts. This seems to have all of the characteristics of a sanction, though it is also a provision for nullification. Notice that though it is the prospect of losing money that is the evil and hence the "real" sanction as far as shopkeepers are concerned,* we cannot say that what the legislature has prescribed as a sanction is not nullity but simply a monetary loss. If that were so, it would be illegal for the shopkeeper to accept money tendered as payment under the contract. But *ex hypothesi* the legislature has not said that he may not receive payment; it has said only that he has no legal claim to it, that he cannot enforce the contract in a court because it is null and void. This is the force of saying that nullity is a sanction: it deprives one of what would otherwise be a legal claim.

But though nullity can be a sanction, nullities are by no means always sanctions. For it is true, as Hart maintains, that if the law provides a way of doing something, there logically must be a way of failing to do it, and a nullity does not necessarily have to be aimed at discouraging or suppressing some kind of prohibited behavior. It may be merely a matter of withholding recognition. In order, then, to determine whether a provision for nullity is a sanction, it must be determined what it is a consequence of. If it is a consequence of the violation of a duty, it is a sanction, and if not, not. Hence, we cannot use, as Hart attempts to do, the dis-

---

* We should assume, for the sake of argument, that there are no other legal remedies, not based on the contract, available to shopkeepers.

tinction between nullity and sanction to help in distinguishing between duty-imposing and power-conferring laws, for we need the latter distinction in order to make the former.[7]

Sanction and Legal Consequence

Not all legally imposed deprivations are sanctions. Legally ordered quarantines, destruction of diseased animals or infested property, and other such deprivations are not sanctions because there is neither violation nor neglect of law by those adversely affected, nor are these evils imposed to enforce obedience. These points are widely accepted. But the point that not all legally imposed deprivations are sanctions can, I think, be pushed into a somewhat more contentious area.

Here in the United States we have just witnessed, in the 1970's, a series of dramatic political events that have raised serious questions about whether there are any sanctions connected with the behavior of Presidents or other officials who fail to uphold their official duties, including the very general duty to uphold the Constitution. There is always the possibility of removal from office for such behavior, and some consider this a sanction, though I will argue that it need not be. (If it is a sanction it does not involve the use of physical force or other sort of coercion; though removing someone from the White House might require physical force, it takes none at all to declare that he is no longer President.) Similarly with regard to other legal consequences of acts violative of official duties: a judge who conducts matters unfairly or acts outside of his authorization may have matters taken out of his hands, or he may be overruled, or the proceedings may be quashed; but these are not sanctions against the official, or at least need not be.

I will give an argument by analogy for the view that a legal consequence such as removal from office need not be a sanction. First, a law may make an alien ineligible for a certain office, but it is clear, I think, that this is not a sanction, even if a person deliberately became an alien by renouncing his citizenship. Such a law has to do entirely with eligibility for office: the aim, whether for good reasons or bad, is to permit only citizens to hold office.

Second, suppose we have a law saying that anyone who has ever failed to fulfill any of the duties of any public office he has held is not eligible for a given office. This loss of eligibility is not, or at least need not be, a sanction for having failed to fulfill official duties, any more than the loss of eligibility for having no claim to citizenship is a sanction; the intent may simply be to try to ensure that sufficiently conscientious or trustworthy persons hold office. Finally, a law that takes away a person's eligibility to hold an office for acts done while he holds that office need be no more a sanction than one that denies eligibility for acts he did prior to holding the office. Indeed, there is an analogy between eligibility and certain nullities: just as wherever there is a way of doing something there logically must be a way of failing to do it, so where there is a way of being eligible for something there logically must be a way of failing to be eligible for it. And just as the question of whether nullity is a sanction or not depends on why it is imposed, so also with ineligibility.

The foregoing kinds of cases, in which the presence or absence of a sanction is not at all clear and depends on why a given adverse legal consequence is imposed, might make us wonder whether intention should be part of the characterization of a sanction, or to put it another way, whether it matters whether a given legal consequence is a sanction or not. What difference does it make, one might ask, whether removal from office is or is not a sanction? After all, the official has legal duties regardless, and the motivating force of the possibility of removal from office is probably the same whether or not it is a sanction. What, if anything, is added if it is imposed for one reason rather than another? Indeed, the same question might be raised for the general case: if what is important is whether the consequence of a particular act will have desired results (discourage noncompliance, cause suffering, or whatever) then what difference does it make whether it is a sanction or something else? The answer is that it can matter both whether a given consequence is officially imposed and whether it is a sanction; it can matter because there are limits to the right of the government to impose sanctions. If something like John Stuart Mill's principle concerning legitimate interference with individual behavior is accepted, then a distinction must be drawn, as Mill saw, between those consequences that are intended to punish (or deter) and those that are not (Mill calls the latter natural consequences).[8] The point is that just as one person's reaction to another's behavior, however damaging to the latter, is not a sanction and hence not subject to Mill's principle if it is a natural reaction and is not aimed at harming, so also official responses, however damaging, are not sanctions and hence not subject to Mill's principle if not intended to punish or discourage. Nullity and ineligibility may be thus analogous to natural consequences, and it makes a difference whether they are or not.

Taxes, Damages, and Sanctions

The state (or the government), through the law, imposes taxes on citizens (and on some non-citizens). It also makes people liable to pay damages to others in certain circumstances. Undoubtedly taxes and damages are burdens imposed on us, and at least to this extent they are similar to sanctions. Some legal thinkers have held, or have had theories of law that imply, that taxes or damages (or both) are themselves sanctions.

Oliver Wendell Holmes and the legal realists thought that the law could profitably be viewed as predictions of what officials of a legal system, in particular judges, will do. For some purposes it may be profitable to view the law in this way; if all that a person wants to know is what will happen to him if he does something, then the predictions of what courts will do will be quite relevant. But viewing laws as predictions is not an adequate theoretical characterization of law because it fails to yield the distinction between a fine and a tax on a course of conduct. The distinction is that if engaging in a course of conduct will result in a fine, then the conduct violates the law; but if a tax is levied the conduct does not violate the law (though, as we shall see, we might have to say that where a tax is levied the conduct *usually* does not violate the law). Fines are connected with legal wrongdoing; taxes are (usually) not. Hence, fines are sanctions whereas taxes are not, even though the point of a tax may be to discourage conduct (such as smoking cigarettes). We must be careful, however, not to conclude that wherever a legally imposed burden is a tax, the conduct to which it is attached is not illegal. Suppose that only the Internal Revenue Service is permitted to examine financial records, and that rather than change this law so as to enable the Federal Bureau of Investigation to acquire information connected with its investigations, the legislature imposes a tax on, say, the proceeds of interstate prostitution. The point of imposing this tax is largely to discourage an (already) illegal activity by giving the IRS access to records; but it is, for all that, a tax and not a fine. So though we can characterize a sanction in terms of the intention to discourage (and/or to punish) illegal behavior, not everything that is so intended need be a sanction. Perhaps this can be worked out by distinguishing the aim or purpose of the (kind of) burden from the intention in imposing it, but it is not clear to me whether this is a tenable distinction. At any rate it is a vague distinction and must be made clearer.

Damages, unlike taxes, do appear to have the character of sanctions, for their purpose may be to discourage certain kinds of wrongdoing. In the traditional theory of damages for breach of contract, ordinary damages (as distinguished from punitive damages) are not thought of in this way. The theory is that the plaintiff is, so far as possible, to be placed in the situation he would have been in had the contract been honored. Compensation for loss incurred due to breach of contract is thus thought of as a part of what Aristotle calls rectificatory or corrective justice, and would be required by principles of justice quite apart from considerations of deterrence. However, this is not incompatible with their also being aimed at discouraging breaches. The same is true of damages in tort, and indeed the deterrence role of damages is more noteworthy in that area.

On what may loosely be called the realist view of law, damages are decidedly not sanctions, for on this theory contractual relations establish no duties whose violations are to be discouraged. Holmes once maintained that "the duty to keep a contract at common law means a prediction that you must pay damages if you do not keep it—and nothing else."[9] The idea embedded in this account of contractual duty is that it is a matter of indifference, as far as the law is concerned, whether a person fulfills his contract or pays damages; there is no more duty to do one than the other. Indeed, some jurisprudential writers have extended this idea to the whole of the law, which is seen not as requiring this or that behavior, but merely as imposing a set of tariffs on certain behavior. Even Blackstone maintained such a view for at least part of the criminal law:

But in relation to those laws which enjoin only *positive duties* and forbid only such things as are not *mala in se*, but *mala prohibita* merely, without any intermixture of moral guilt, annexing a penalty to non-compliance; here I apprehend conscience is no farther concerned, than by directing a submission to the penalty, in case of our breach of those laws. ... [I]n these cases the alternative is offered to every man; "either abstain from this, or submit to such a penalty"; and his conscience will be clear, whichever side of the alternative he thinks proper to embrace.[10]

As a theory of law in general this view is quite implausible. The criminal law cannot seriously be taken to be indifferent to the commission of rapes, for example, so long as the rapist pays the price. To be sure, we have recently heard it said, in connection with civil disobedience, that certain violations are justifiable if one accepts the penalty, but despite such claims the criminal law cannot seriously be taken as offering such choices. The view is implausible even with regard to most of the laws that are *mala prohibita* and not *mala in se* (e.g. most traffic or hunting laws). As a theory of contracts the view is no better, as the existence and appropriateness of the remedy of specific performance makes clear. For if the law of contracts does permit a person the choice of fulfilling his contract or paying money damages it would hardly be in place for a court to require a breaching party to fulfill his contract as written.

Assuming that damages are at least sometimes sanctions, are all ordinary damages sanctions? Sometimes they do serve to discourage; for example, the possibility of having to pay damages makes more careful drivers out of most of us. But suppose I enter into a contract with Jones to have some work done on my house, and then I do not pay him for the job. He may sue to recover, as damages for breach of contract, the agreed-upon price. But the possibility of having to pay damages of this sort cannot serve to discourage my breach, and thus cannot seriously be intended to do so, for I would have had to pay the same amount anyway. (The lawsuit may be time-consuming and expensive, and this may discourage my breach, but then this and not the damages constitutes the sanction, if anything does.) Of course, though punitive damages are not permitted in the ordinary breach of contract case, Jones may suffer other losses as a result of my breach, and the possibility of having to pay additional damages may discourage my breach. But since the main element of damages in this particular case is not a sanction, it follows that not all damages are to be understood as sanctions.

Nevertheless, it seems fairly clear that sometimes damages are correctly viewed, at least in part, as sanctions. This seems to require, though, as with all sanctions, that we think of their aim or purpose as being to discourage (or to punish). But how is this aim or purpose to be ascertained? One way of ascertaining it would be to find such an intent in a preamble to a statute or in the transcripts of legislative deliberations or the like (though there are serious difficulties in trying to locate clear legislative intentions in such materials). But the law regarding damages is often not statutory, and as a result we cannot always refer the aim or purpose of some legally imposed burden to the intentions of some person or body. We could of course hold that it makes no sense, at least where there are no discoverable intentions, to talk about the aim or purpose of a legal burden; but to do this, it seems to me, is to give up the attempt to make the important distinction between those adverse legal consequences that are sanctions and those that are not. A possible way to deal with the characterization of sanctions, and one that seems to me quite plausible, is to think in terms of possible legal justifications for imposing certain burdens, as a way of getting at their aim or purpose. If there is a principle of law that supports the imposition of a burden for some wrongdoing, then we can maintain that the aim or purpose of the burden is to attain whatever the principle seeks to attain.* This does not imply that the imposition of the burden has an adequate legal justification.

COERCION IN THE LAW

Force, Coercion, and Sanction

Threats of dismissal from one's job, loss of credit, disclosure of damaging information, loss of a business license, loss of welfare payments, and loss of the privilege of driving a car are only a few examples of ways of coercing without using force. The use of coercive sanctions therefore does not necessarily involve the threat of physical force. This point partially undermines theories of law that insist on a tight connection between law and force. Both Austin and Kelsen are in this camp; both hold that every directive (command in Austin's theory, norm in Kelsen's) in a legal system must be connected with force. For Austin, a law is a command backed up by a threat of force; for Kelsen it is a norm that directs an official to apply force under certain circumstances.

But even if coercive sanctions do not in all cases involve force, could there not still be a tight connection, of the kind maintained by Austin and Kelsen, between law and coercive sanction? If some of the points made earlier in this chapter, in our discussion of sanctions and legal consequences, are correct, we would have to say no, for there are duties of officials in a legal system that are not enforced by sanctions. Legal consequences such as removal from office need not be sanctions.

Still, the use of coercive sanctions in national legal systems is quite notable, and even if sanctions are not logically connected with each and every law, many theorists have thought that coercive sanctions are indeed necessary features of law, and that a completely adequate theory of law must take note of the role they

* Note that this merely suggests how we might understand the notion of the aims or purposes of burdens that are imposed on us. It does not yet say how the aim of (imposing) a sanction is to be distinguished from the aim of (imposing) a tax, and hence does not solve the problem raised a few pages earlier in connection with the distinction between a tax and a fine.

play. I too think that there is an important sense in which the law must employ coercive sanctions, or at least be prepared to do so. I will use Hart's views on this matter as a vehicle for bringing out these points.

Hart maintains that there are certain things about which a legal system must, as a matter of "natural" but not logical necessity, have something to say. For example, a legal system must restrict the use of violence because human beings are normally vulnerable to and sometimes subject to bodily attack. But this is so, he says, only because human beings are constructed as they are; if they were constructed differently they might not be able to attack others or be vulnerable to attack by others. Thus, if law must have a certain minimal content, this is due to contingencies of nature and not to the concept of law. Hart's view of the sense in which sanctions are required is similar: sanctions are required as a matter of natural but not logical necessity.

Though most of what Hart has to say on this matter is correct, there are other points to bring out that to some extent alter his conclusion. These points were made earlier in connection with the natural law theory discussed in Chapter 5.[11] What I argued there was that the law must, logically, have some content or other, that apparently the only possibilities for what a legal system might deal with are the resolution or regulation of conflict and the expanding, via power-conferring laws, of possibilities for what people can do or bring about, and that of these the former is the irreducible minimum that a legal system deals with.

If law has to do with at least the resolution or regulation of conflict, then there can be law only where there is the possibility of conflict among the individuals to whom the law is to apply. Now according to Hart, it is a contingent fact that human beings are constructed as they are, and for this reason the concept of law is not to be taken to require, logically, that there be, for example, restrictions on the use of violence. Hart is perhaps correct in saying that the concept of law does not itself logically require restrictions on the use of violence, but he is mistaken about the reason. The proper reason, as I see it, is that the concept of law can apply to beings other than human beings, as long as they have the capacity to understand and to follow rules. Seen in this way, the concept of law plainly does not have to do, directly, with the contingencies of human construction. But this does not mean that the concept of law is wholly content-neutral. The concept of law can have a place only where there are individuals, human or otherwise, among whom there is the possibility of conflict, and it is this that makes it correct to say that the concept of law has to do, logically, with conflicts and their resolution or regulation.

Of course, the way in which conflicts are dealt with depends on the characteristics of the beings to whom the law is to apply. Among human beings there is, obviously, the possibility of conflict; constructed as they are, for example, human beings are vulnerable to attack. So though Hart is correct in saying that human legal systems must include rules dealing with the use of violence, and also in saying that this is not logically required by the concept of law itself, he is mistaken in thinking that there is no connection between the need for such rules and the concept of law. For the concept of law requires that there be rules dealing with conflicts, whatever the sorts of conflicts that can arise among different sorts of beings.

Nothing that has been said so far has to do with coercive sanctions. For though the law must, logically, have rules dealing with conflicts, it need not, logically, employ coercive sanctions in order to bring about conforming behavior. But the argument suggests the following, which is, I think, logically true of law. If the beings whose behavior is regulated by a legal system are such that some manipulative devices are (non-logically) required if there is to be compliance, then the legal system must (logically) provide such devices. Now this does not yet yield the stronger conclusion that a legal system that regulates the behavior of humans must (logically) employ coercive sanctions, for there may be other devices for promoting compliance. And, indeed, that conclusion cannot be reached just from an examination of the concept of law. So the question is what this weaker claim—that devices for promoting compliance must (logically) be provided if compliance is not otherwise forthcoming—implies for a characterization of the nature of a legal system.

Law, Sanction, and Ideology

Oberdiek maintains that the dominant characteristic of law is that it promotes freedom rather than restricting it. Law is liberating in two ways: (1) it protects its subjects from harm, and protects and secures their rights, liberties, powers, economic opportunities, and bases of self-respect; and (2) it augments their powers by various legal instruments, such as contracts and wills, which make it possible to do what could not otherwise be done.* All of this is not a simple matter of there being power-conferring laws, says Oberdiek; it is rather that legal systems are *"structures within which men can refine, develop, and augment their capacities and powers—for good or evil. The latter description leaves open the possibility that, in ordering human relationships, law may promote freedom rather than merely restrict it."* [12] We should look forward, then, he thinks, to a legal system that "can provide us with a noncoercive structure for arranging human affairs, a structure minimizing the use of sanctions, coercive or otherwise, and maximizing the use of promotional devices." [13] On the face of it, this would seem to be an elevating picture of the possibilities of legal institutions and an ideal worth working toward. It amounts to no less than looking forward to, and searching for methods for bringing about, a state of affairs in which people respond to reasons for compliance other than coercive sanctions.

Among the promotional devices that might be employed, economic incentives would undoubtedly be very important. Such incentives are used now in our own legal system to encourage businesses to locate in certain areas, make capital investments, and the like. Tax advantages are offered to individuals to encourage

---

* In the light of the liberating character of power-conferring laws, the fact that most nullities are not sanctions (see pp. 142–46) takes on special importance.

them to purchase houses, rewards are offered for information about crimes, and medals are given for certain kinds of behavior. Undoubtedly these are effective ways of encouraging desired behavior. But however desirable such promotional devices are, we must not too quickly conclude that a thoroughgoing system of promotional devices would be a good thing, which is to say, that we should get rid of coercive ("negative") sanctions in favor of rewards or "positive" sanctions.

The law discourages or provides disincentives by saying to the individual, in effect, "If you do *a*, then you must submit to *b*." The formula for positive sanctions, on the other hand, is "If you do *a*, you have a claim to *b*." These two formulas for the legal techniques of using sanctions are Norberto Bobbio's, who interprets them this way: "The fundamental nature of a measure of discouragement is a threat, but the fundamental nature of an encouragement measure is a promise."[14] Now in order for something to be a reward—that is, in order for it to be something that is offered rather than threatened—it must be something to which the offeree is not already entitled and which the offeror is not already bound to give. Entitlement must be seen as arising from, and only from, the offeree's doing (or refraining from doing) the act for which the reward is to be given. This implies that the offeror has the right to control what is being offered as a reward, and that the offeree has no rights with respect to it until the offer is made and accepted. But though this may be an acceptable state of affairs with respect to tax advantages, medals, and the like, it would be quite worrisome (to say the least) if the law was in a position to offer freedom from confinement, or the opportunity to vote, or food and medical care, as rewards for the desired behavior.

There might be quite acceptable techniques for, say, reducing the crime rate that do not involve sanctions. But straightforward sanctions are important not only because of whatever effectiveness they have, but because the use of sanctions bespeaks a political ideology in which a natural right to liberty is recognized by the state. From the standpoint of such an ideology it is all-important that the state confronts the individual, with respect to certain matters at any rate, as threatening evil rather than as bearing gifts. For to do the former is to threaten to take away something to which one is otherwise entitled, while to do the latter is to offer something to which one is *not* otherwise entitled.

How, in the end, shall we characterize law? Shall we regard it as "necessarily, universally, or by nature coercive," or as necessarily, universally, or by nature liberating and promotional? Or is neither of these any more the dominant character of the law than the other? On the one hand, stimulating socially desirable behavior and social change may be a good thing, and if it is, the law must inevitably be an important part of the mechanism to that end. But this does not mean that the law is to be viewed as essentially a liberating and promotional institution. As Bobbio points out, we must separate our legal theory and our ideology.[15] On the other hand, I have argued that a legal system must (logically) provide devices for bringing about compliance if it is not otherwise forthcoming. If human beings behave often enough in certain ways, then ideologically acceptable promotional devices might do the job (though this would not be their only job); if humans do not so behave, then coercive sanctions might have to be employed. As things are, coercive sanctions do seem to be required. But more important, unless human nature were to become significantly altered, it would appear that a legal system must always be prepared to employ coercive sanctions—that is, to create standing reasons of a certain sort for compliance should other reasons or motivations fail. It is for this reason that coercive sanctions must be looked on as indispensable to an adequate account of human law.

8

Legal Rights

In 1913 and 1917 Wesley Newcomb Hohfeld, of Yale Law School, published the two parts of his "Fundamental Legal Conceptions as Applied in Judicial Reasoning." Hohfeld's aim was to illuminate a variety of legal problems by showing how they could be reduced to certain fundamental legal relations. This was not a new aim in the law, as Hohfeld indicates in referring to "the express or tacit assumption that all legal relations may be reduced to 'rights' and 'duties'."[1] The problem, the hindrance to the "clear understanding," the "incisive statement," and the "true solution" of legal problems, according to Hohfeld, is the express or tacit assumption that reducing legal relations to those two categories is "adequate for the purpose of analyzing even the most complex interests, such as trusts, options, escrows, 'future' interests, corporate interests, etc."[2] What Hohfeld sought to provide was a set of fundamental, *sui generis*, legal relations adequate for the purpose of explaining complex legal arrangements.

Hohfeld distinguishes four kinds of legal right (or senses of the term right), and exhibits their logical relations. These are claim-right (which is a right in the strict sense); liberty (Hohfeld called it a privilege; permission is another term that is close to it); power; and immunity. These are most easily explained by means of examples. If I lend you twenty dollars, then I have a right (a claim-right) against you for twenty dollars. If I see twenty dollars laying in the street, I have a right (am at liberty) to pick it up, though I have no right (claim-right) to the twenty dollars from you if you pick it up first. If I wish to do so, I can make you the owner of twenty dollars of mine; I have the legal power to do this—that is, there are acts I can perform that have the effect of changing the legal relations between us. Once I give you the twenty dollars, however, I can no longer do things unilaterally that alter your legal interest in the money; you have an immunity against my doing so.

It is important to notice that in a given situation or transaction we can have more than one of these kinds of rights. Indeed, we can have all of them at the same time. If you owe me money, I have a right (claim-right) against you for the money, I have the right (am at liberty) to accept money tendered as payment, I have the right (power) to forgive the debt, and I have the right to the non-alteration of (i.e., I have an immunity against the alteration of) my legal situation by you or anyone else, including, for the most part, the government. Again, the owner of a piece of land has a right (claim-right) against others entering, a right (liberty) to enter, a right (power) to allow others to enter, and a right (immunity) against others unilaterally exercising powers that would alter these and other legal relations.

Each of these rights, or senses of "right," has, according to Hohfeld, an opposite (or contradictory) and a correlative, as follows: [3]

Jural opposites		Jural correlatives	
right	no-right	right	duty
privilege	duty	privilege	no-right
power	disability	power	liability
immunity	liability	immunity	disability

The relation of correlativity is explained as follows. If *A* has a right to *B*'s doing *x* (e.g. pay twenty dollars as agreed), then *B* has a duty to *A* to do *x*. Right and duty are two sides of the same relation. Similarly, *A*'s privilege (liberty) as against *B* to do *x* (e.g. pick up twenty dollars from the street) correlates with *B*'s no-right (i.e. *B*'s not having a right) that *A* not do *x*. The relation of opposition is simply that of logical contradiction. If *A* has a right to *B*'s doing *x*, this is the contradictory of *A*'s having no right (a no-right) to *B*'s doing *x*. And if *A* is at liberty, as against *B*, to do *x*, then this is the contradictory of *A*'s having a duty to *B* not to do *x*. Analogous relations obtain among powers, liabilities, disabilities, and immunities.

Hohfeld's relations are a bit more difficult to understand, however, than the symmetry of his tables suggests. The problem is that it is necessary, at certain points, to insert negations in order to state the relations correctly. For example, my liberty to do *x* is not the opposite of my duty to do *x*, but of my duty *not* to do *x*,* and the correlative of your having no right to my doing *x* is not my liberty to do *x*, but my liberty *not* to do *x*. The relations can very nicely be set out in squares of opposition, though because of the problem of negations there are really two sets of relations for each interrelated set of terms. How this works for one of the sets of terms is shown in the following diagram:

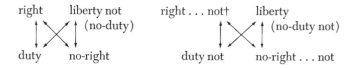

The vertical arrows indicate the relation of correlativity, and the diagonal arrows the relation of opposition. Glanville Williams suggests thinking of the diagonals as expressing what happens when a right or a duty is repealed or its existence is denied. If, for example, I have a duty to pay taxes, and the tax statutes are repealed, I have a liberty not to pay taxes, and so on for the other diagonals, working either from left to right or from right to left.[4]

The idea that there is a logical correlation between rights and duties will be investigated in this chapter, so we might well begin

---

* Hohfeld himself adverts to this point: "[A]lways, when it is said that a given privilege is the mere negation of a *duty*, what is meant, of course, is a duty having a content or tenor precisely *opposite* to that of the privilege in question" (*Fundamental Legal Conceptions as Applied in Judicial Reasoning*, ed. W. W. Cook, New Haven, Conn., 1964, p. 39). Italics in original.

† That is, right that another shall not.

by summarizing Hohfeld's views on the subject, and some of their implications. Hohfeld sees the fundamental pattern of legal relations as triadic, involving two individuals and one act. Rights are always against someone, and duties are always owed to someone. Even liberties are always liberties as against some individual.

On Hohfeld's view one does not have a legal relation with more than one person; if there are other individuals involved, one has separate legal relations with each. Arthur Corbin, explaining Hohfeld, says: "A so-called legal relation to the State or to a corporation may always be reduced to many legal relations with the individuals composing the State or the corporation, even though for convenient discussion they may be grouped."[5] This way of conceiving legal rights also shows up in Hohfeld's conception of the distinction between special and general rights (*in personam* and *in rem* rights). Holding that "since the purpose of the law is to regulate the conduct of human beings, all jural relations must, in order to be clear and direct in their meaning, be predicated of such human beings,"[6] Hohfeld considers *in rem* rights to be merely packages of *in personam* rights:

[A right *in personam*] is either a unique right residing in a person (or group of persons) and availing against a single person (or single group of persons); or else it is one of a *few* fundamentally similar, yet separate, rights availing respectively against a few definite persons. [A right *in rem*] is always *one* of a large *class* of *fundamentally similar* yet separate rights, actual and potential, residing in a *single* person . . . but availing *respectively* against persons constituting a very large and indefinite class of people.[7]

Hohfeld thus stands as an exponent of a strong form of what is called the thesis of the logical correlativity of rights and duties. For he holds that for every right there is a correlative duty, and for every duty a correlative right. This thesis is of course to be distinguished from the *moral* thesis that rights and duties are correlatives in the sense that a being cannot have rights unless it has and fulfills its duties, and also from the thesis that a person who fails to fulfill certain of his duties thereby forfeits certain of his rights.

LIBERTIES AND THE DUTY NOT TO INTERFERE

Is the correlativity thesis correct for legal rights? Before we try to answer this, let us examine the contention of some philosophers that there is a relation of correlativity not only between claim-rights and duties, but between liberties and duties. The idea is that liberties are correlatives of, and indeed can be explained in terms of, the duties of others not to interfere. For example, my liberty to pick up twenty dollars lying on the ground, or to speak freely, is a matter of others having duties not to interfere with my doing these things. It seems to me that this analysis of liberties is mistaken—or, in other words, that permission is a logically independent norm-character.

Suppose liberties were reducible to duties not to interfere. Then A's liberty to do x is equivalent to B's duty not to interfere with A, and this, by the correlativity thesis, is equivalent to A's right to B's noninterference. That is, to have a liberty is equivalent to having a claim-right to the noninterference of others. But then, contrary to what has been asserted previously, liberties are merely a subclass of claim-rights, not something separate and different from them.

If this argument is not sufficient, there is another, stronger argument against the attempt to reduce liberties to duties not to interfere. First of all, a permission to do x cannot just be (or even imply) a prohibition against all interferences with the doing of x, for some kinds of interference are not impermissible. I may, for example, deliberately prevent you from picking up the twenty dollars in the street, or from expressing yourself freely, by diverting your attention; and in hockey a player is permitted to interfere in more violent ways with the movements of certain of his opponents. But further, a permission to do x is not merely the sum of prohibitions against assault, fraud, intimidation, and so forth, or even the sum of prohibitions against preventing others from doing x by assault, fraud, and so forth—for even if these prohibitions exist it may still be wrong for a person to do x. For example, gambling may be illegal, but a legislature may have some reason for making a special prohibition against a private citizen forcibly breaking up a gambling game (such a law might be needed to combat vigilante activities). This prohibition on certain interferences with gambling does not amount to or entail a permission to gamble—gambling is still illegal.

Let us consider another possible way of expressing liberties as duties not to interfere. The argument might go as follows. If my having a liberty is a matter of my doing no wrong in doing x, this amounts to saying that I am not to be held liable in any way for doing x. That is, the courts and other officials are not to interfere with my doing x by holding me liable for doing it. So to say that I have a liberty is to say that the courts have a duty not to interfere. This argument will not do, however. The duty of the courts not to interfere is not sufficient for one's having a liberty, for one's being prohibited from doing x is compatible with there being no court having jurisdiction to deal with x. For example, if *Marbury* v. *Madison* had gone the other way and held that the courts could not review certain legislative acts in order to determine whether they are within Constitutional limits, it would nevertheless not be permissible for the legislature to ignore those Constitutional limits. Likewise, if a sloppy legislature were to get rid of one class of courts, not realizing that they were the only courts with jurisdiction to deal with a given matter, this would not constitute a permission to do what had heretofore been prohibited. (There are affinities between this and an aspect of the legal situation in the Nuremberg trials. The prosecution argued that defendants' acts were prohibited even though there was at the time no mechanism for enforcement. The defendants argued in effect that the absence of such mechanisms meant that their acts were not legally prohibited at the time. Whatever we think of the prosecution's claim that the acts were legally prohibited when done, it was surely right on the logical point that lack of legal capacity to deal with certain matters does not imply that they are not prohibited.)

Apparently, though, the duty of courts not to interfere is necessary if one is to have a liberty. For how could I be at liberty to do x (i.e. have no duty not to do x, so that I would be doing no wrong in doing x) if officials could legitimately interfere with my doing x?

But though there is something worth paying attention to here, it does not establish an important connection between liberties and duties not to interfere. First of all, if I am at liberty to do x, officials do not (usually) have a duty imposed on them not to interfere with my doing x in the way that one might have a duty not to interfere in certain ways with, say, others' contractual relationships. Rather, officials typically lack the authority, capacity, or competence to interfere where a citizen has a liberty. So when I have a liberty to do x, this connects with the legal authorization of officials with respect to my doing x, and not, strictly speaking, with specific duties imposed on officials. Of course, officials do have the legal duty to act only within their authority, but it is implausible to regard this duty as the one with which my liberty correlates, for this would amount to saying that my liberty to do x correlates with the duty of officials to be law-abiding.

RIGHTS AND DUTIES

To return now to the thesis of the correlativity of claim-rights and duties, that thesis seems to me to be doubtful, at least from the side of the duties. A citizen has many duties of obedience that he owes to no one in particular, and the performance of which no one in particular has a right to—for example, the duty to stop at a traffic signal or to pay taxes.[8] But the correlativity thesis is widely taken to hold up when viewed from the side of the claim-rights: wherever there is a legal right there appears to be a correlative duty that another individual owes to the rightholder.

What kind of account of legal rights might be given if the correlativity thesis is correct, or at least substantially correct? One suggestion is that to have a right is just to stand to benefit from the performance of a duty. But without qualification, this is quite inadequate; for example, if you owe me money, which I mean to give to charity when you pay me, the charity stands to benefit from your satisfying your obligation, but it has no right to it. An improved version of the benefit theory avoids this by saying (in part) that to have a right is to be the "direct, intended beneficiary" of a duty or obligation; it is to be an individual who is "supposed to benefit" from the obligation.[9] There is, however, a difficulty even with this qualified version of the benefit theory—the problem of the third party beneficiary. If I promise you that I will look after your cat while you are away, the cat is the intended beneficiary, but you, and not the cat, have the right to my performance.

Hart gives an alternative account of rights, one that avoids this problem and at the same time deals with what he takes to be a further and quite important matter. Hart worries that an account of legal rights solely in terms of being the beneficiary of a legal duty of a certain kind makes the notion of a legal right superfluous, since "all that can be said in a terminology of such rights can be and indeed is best said in the indispensable terminology of duty."[10] In particular, Hart insists that an individual's rights under civil law and also with respect to many public welfare functions of government amount to something more than merely being the intended beneficiary of a duty. What rightholders have that is of additional importance is a legally respected choice. Such a rightholder can usually waive the duty, "enforce" it by suing for compensation, injunction, and the like, and waive the duty to make reparation. These are special powers that a rightholder has, and it is the presence of these powers that is important about legal rights, and that the intended beneficiary theory misses. Rights are things we can exercise. Such a view of legal rights does not, however, account for most of the rights in the criminal law, such as the right not to be murdered or assaulted, and Hart concedes that the concept of a right is superfluous here. Many years ago John Chipman Gray maintained a similar view:

The legal rights of a man are the rights which are exercisable on his motion. A man has, therefore, no legal right as to those interests in the realizing of which he is protected only by other people exercising their rights. The fact that the State can punish the burglar who breaks into my house does not give *me* any right not to have my house broken into.[11]

(Gray holds, nevertheless, that the citizen does in fact have a right not to have his house broken into—because the law permits him to resist and to place obstacles in the burglar's way. His view, like Hart's, is roughly that there is a legal right only where there is

something that one may do on his own choice.) Hart does hold,
though, that there are legal rights, albeit of a different sort, when
it comes to fundamental or constitutional rights. Where there is a
constitutional right to associate or to speak freely, this amounts to
a limitation on legislative authority, and hence to an immunity
from such legislative acts. Hart's view in sum, then, is that the
central notion of a legal right, exemplified primarily in the civil
law, is that of a legally respected choice. Talk of rights in criminal
law is for the most part a redundant and useless translation of the
duties of the criminal law into the terminology of rights, except
where there is a constitutional dimension, in which case the rights
are not claim-rights but immunity-rights.

One reply to the contention that talk about rights in the criminal
law is a redundant and useless translation of talk about duties is
provided by David Braybrooke.[12] Rights and duties are correlative,
he maintains, but the correlation is not a neat and tidy one, for the
concept of a right is open-textured, and so is the concept of the
obligation that correlates with it. What this means is that it is not
always clear just which duties correlate with a right, and that the
duties that correlate with a right are subject to change. So even if
rights are logically superfluous—indeed even if they are practically
superfluous in the sense that people heed their obligations anyway—the concept of a right is a useful one. Braybrooke is not
perfectly clear on this point, but from his remarks about open-
texture I would guess that he sees rights as useful in that they help
us to determine which new duties should be recognized and
imposed as social conditions change. This implies, however, that
the concept of a right has some independent content that is not
exhausted by reference to correlative duties, for without this it is
not clear how rights could be useful in the way I take Braybrooke
to be suggesting. Braybrooke does not offer anything in connection
with this—but, then, that was not his aim.

Though Braybrooke has not told us the whole story, he has
sensed that on the stricter or tidier correlativity thesis, rights do
not seem to be as important as we are generally inclined to think
they are. That is just the right difficulty to raise, I believe, against

Hart's claim that rights under the criminal law are reducible to correlative duties, for in the crucial areas in which rights are asserted—such as in policy formation and in judicial decision-making—his view does not give any greater weight to rights than to their correlative duties, and certainly does not provide a decision-maker with grounds for imposing new duties. Hart does regard rights in civil law as not being reducible to correlative duties in that they involve powers, but nevertheless when it comes to their role in policy formation and judicial decision-making these powers add nothing, and the weight of the rights is carried wholly by their correlative duties. Hart does, to be sure, recognize a special role for fundamental, constitutional rights, but this is due to their being rights of a different sort—immunity-rights.

This point of Hart's provides a good place to begin a reply. Hart is quite correct in noting that some rights involve immunities from governmental action—e.g. the right of free speech. This right is not just a liberty; it is not merely that a person does no wrong in saying what he wants. What is special about this right is that our having it means that government officials may not infringe it if they think, even correctly, that it would be better if we did not exercise it on some occasion. But Hart seems to say that this is *the* kind of right that the right to free speech is; he seems to suppose that different rights have different and mutually exclusive roles. This does not seem to me to be correct, for rights like the right of free speech could serve not only to impose disabilities on the government,[13] but also to support directly injunctions against private individuals or private damage suits.[14] This has two implications that are damaging for Hart's view. First, these private suits need not concern any acts of the government, so the right of free speech cannot be just an immunity from certain governmental acts. Is the right in these cases reducible to the duties of others? Can we say something to the effect that in some of its aspects the right of free speech is an immunity from governmental acts and not reducible to duties, whereas in other aspects it is reducible to duties? The difficulty with these suggestions is that one and the same right is involved in both instances, and furthermore it seems to be distinguishable from both the immunity and the duties of others, and even from both of these together. Second, legal rights have a role in creating legal duties. If the judiciary were to enjoin certain interferences with public addresses by appeal to the right of free speech, such a ruling would be in effect the creation of a new legal duty, though it would not be the creation of a new legal right. Hence the right cannot be taken to be the correlative of the legal duty, for the right existed when the duty did not.

Let me amplify some of these points having to do with rights as involved in the creation of duties. Prohibitions in the law usually come in the form of fairly narrow legal rules that say what behavior is prescribed and what legal remedies are available to deal with it. There are also in a legal system a variety of general principles that judges can use to extend existing rules for an unforeseen situation or to formulate new ones. Rules and principles differ in two ways. First, rules but not principles apply in an all-or-nothing fashion: if the conditions set out by a rule of law are satisfied, then the rule must be applied unless it is to be changed by making an exception to it. A principle, on the other hand, supplies a reason to be taken into account, and has a dimension of weight or importance that rules lack. A principle does not require a particular outcome, for it may be outweighed by other principles. However, its being outweighed does not mean that it has been changed; no exception has been made to it. [15]

Now though legal duties are most often contained in rules, legal rights have their most significant roles at the level of principles. True, principles can and sometimes do refer to duties (for example, "Car manufacturers have a duty to protect the public from accidents"). But for one thing, a duty like this is easily expressible in terms of the rights of car buyers, and for another, at the level of principles it is the goals of a legal system that are being expressed, and the goals of law are most appropriately viewed as a matter of protecting and promoting certain interests rather than as a matter of imposing duties on certain classes of individuals. Since most often a person's right is secured by getting another person to do or refrain from doing certain things, it is natural to expect duties rather than rights to be most visible at the level at which the working law has regular impact on people—i.e. at the level of rules. If this is an appropriate way of looking at one division of labor in a legal system, then the question of whether rights can be reduced to duties is closely related to the question of whether principles and rules are really distinct sorts of things—whether, that is, principles can be reduced to rules. But though a court's reference to a principle—such as the principle that every person has a right to personal security—may sometimes be simply a summary reference to a variety of legal rules, [16] very often judges do in fact have resort to independent legal standards that have special force in the interpretation of rules of law, in the making of exceptions to rules of law, in the overruling of rules of law and the making of new ones. To say then that legal rights have a role in the creation of legal duties is closely connected with the point made here, that legal principles have a role in the creation or modification of legal rules, and in neither case is the one reducible to the other. This is exhibited quite clearly in connection with the right to privacy, where, starting around the beginning of this century, the explicit recognition of the right to privacy as a principle of law preceded and served as the justification for the development of common law rules designed to protect privacy. [17]

SPECIAL RIGHTS AND THE CORRELATIVITY THESIS

There are, I think, reasons for driving a wedge between rights and claims with regard to special as well as general rights—that is, reasons for denying that even special rights are to be viewed as rights against someone. Suppose that Jones and Smith have entered into a contract under which Smith is to provide certain services for a thousand dollars. Jones dies before paying. On the view in question the right no longer exists, for that right was against Jones, and there is no more Jones. Of course, there are rules of law under which someone else acquires a duty to pay Smith, but on the view in question this is a different right. However, this situation is much more naturally described in a different way. Smith's right is one thing, and the claims by which it is supported are something quite different. So when Jones dies, Smith's right does not vanish, to be replaced by another; rather, he has the same right (the right to one thousand dollars under the contract) but supported by a claim against someone else. The claims are unified by the right.[18]

Let me try to shore up this argument against one objection. Why not simply say that Smith *had* a right against Jones in view of which he now has a (different) right against Jones's estate? Now first of all, even though this way of describing things does have a natural ring to it, it is not demanded, and the alternative I am proposing not only sounds plausible but has the additional virtue of being in line with the earlier argument. Second, I think there is something further to be said against the objection. As in the earlier argument, I take rights to constitute reasons for judicial decisions —in particular, reasons for recognizing or rejecting certain claims or defenses. In the objection, by contrast, what is being maintained is that the past existence of one right (r_1: Smith's right against Jones) constitutes a reason for creating another and different right (r_2: Smith's right against Jones's estate). But it would seem, to the contrary, that the ground for creating r_2 is constituted not, as it were, by the whole of r_1, but rather by only one aspect of it: namely, the aspect of protecting Smith's interest as distinguished from the aspect of being against Jones. It seems to me to be more perspicuous, however, to identify the right with the interest straightaway, for this seems to be the only way (or at least the most straightforward way) of preserving the notion that people's rights can sometimes constitute the legal reasons for certain decisions.

The foregoing argument for driving a wedge between rights and claims is not without substantive impact. Take, for example, the concern in recent years with the doctrine of the holder in due course. Suppose you make an installment purchase of an appliance and sign a note for the money owed. If something goes wrong with the appliance that the seller is required by his warranty to fix, but he does not give satisfaction, the outstanding payments provide the buyer with some leverage against the seller, and if the product is hopelessly defective the buyer might be spared having to continue paying. But if the seller transfers the note to another party, then the latter, being a holder in due course, takes the note free of any claims the buyer has against the seller—so that even if the product is no good the buyer must continue paying on the note. Now, if the law alters the position of the holder in due course in such a way that one who buys certain notes takes subject to certain warranty provisions,* it seems more to the point to say that the law is providing a new way of protecting the warranty rights of buyers, rather than that new rights are being created. It is quite an important matter whether we think of the situation in one way or the other; for if a buyer is regarded only as having rights against someone or other rather than as having warranty rights (full stop) that are in need of protection, then the judiciary would be hard put to explain the legal grounds for any modification of the holder in due course doctrine. After all, the buyer has not entered into any special transaction with the new noteholder, so what could justify the creation of new defenses against the latter unless it is the buyer's warranty rights?

The second argument for driving a wedge between special rights and claims is related to the first. In some situations expressing a right as against someone and for something can be ambiguous. As an example, compare the positions of a licensee and the owner of an easement. If I have an easement over your property, I have, on the view in question, a right against you to enter the land. If instead you have given me a license to enter, I again have a right against you to enter the land. But these rights are importantly different. If I have an easement my right is against you, but in a way that is incidental, for the right exists against anyone who comes to own the land. If I have only a license, however, the right is against you in a more essential way: it is only against you, and it remains a

---

* See, for example, Unico v. Owen, 50 N.J. 101, 232 A.2d 405 (1967). "Such contracts, particularly those of the type involved in this case, are so fraught with opportunities for misuse that the purchasers must be protected against oppressive and unconscionable clauses.... We see in the enactment of these two sections of the Code an intention to leave in the hands of the courts the continued application of common law principles in deciding in consumer goods cases whether such waiver clauses as the one imposed on Owen in this case are so one-sided as to be contrary to public policy." (232 A.2d, at 418.)

right only against you even if you dispose of the land. For if there is an easement the new owner takes subject to my right to enter, but if there is only a license he does not; then my only redress is against the licensor, not against the new owner. What we have here is a distinction between a right to property and a right against an individual. And the problem is that the view that rights are (always) against someone and for something does not bring out this distinction. This is an important distinction, however, for it marks a difference between two ways of dealing with property. Where rights are only against individuals (as in the case of a license), property is more easily transferrable. Where rights are rights to property, on the other hand, individual security is promoted at the expense of fluidity, and this bespeaks different social values.[19] Similar remarks may be made with respect to the holder in due course doctrine. Where warranty rights follow the indebtedness, economic fluidity is slowed down in favor of certain kinds of individual security; where they do not, market flexibility is aided at the expense of individual security. This, too (albeit somewhat misleadingly), can be characterized as a matter of whether the rights involved are rights against individuals or rights to property.

There is an objection to this argument that must be met—namely, that the right of the holder of an easement is not properly expressed as a right against, say, Jones to enter Jones's land, but as a right against the owner of the land. Thus when Jones owns it my right is against Jones, and when Smith owns it my right is against Smith, but whoever the land belongs to, I have exactly the same right—a right against the owner of the land. Thus is the correlativity thesis said to be preserved.

This might be a possible way out, but it does not strike me as entirely plausible, for it seems to alter the character of the correlativity thesis, and indeed to weaken it. On the correlativity thesis in its strongest form, to have a right is to stand in a personal relationship to some other, nameable individual. But according to the suggestion now being considered, an easement-right is either a series of relations to a succession of individuals or a relation between a person and a role. But neither of these seems entirely satisfactory, for it is possible (in a possible legal system, at any rate) for there to be a break in the series or for a role to be unoccupied without the right being in the least affected. Suppose that when an owner dies intestate his land becomes unowned, though protected by the state until, by legally prescribed means such as homesteading, it again becomes owned. There is no reason why I could not have an easement over the land during the period that the land is unowned, and yet there is no owner against whom I have this right. More important, suppose that a law is passed providing for interim non-ownership of the sort just described, except that no provision is made for easements, and it falls to the courts to decide that issue. If an easement-right is a right against the owner of the land, then how could any rights of the holder of the easement enter into a court's decision? Yet it seems to me that the easement holder has rights that should have weight in the decision. Hence the right that an easement holder has must be regarded as a right to property and not as a right against someone or other.

I have not intended to imply in the foregoing arguments concerning special rights that distinguishing between rights and claims logically necessitates the distinction between rights to property and rights against individuals. Rather the point is that this distinction and probably others like it exist, that it is an important distinction, and that driving a wedge between rights and claims, and thinking instead of legal rights as protected by and as unifying a variety of claims has two decided advantages. In the first place, it is a more natural way of talking and thinking. But beyond that, as we have seen, it helps to illuminate some matters of social importance.

RIGHTS, REASONS, AND CLAIMS

If rights are not to be understood as being against someone and for something, then what are they? It seems to me that the character of legal rights derives not from the everyday interchanges among people, but from the non-ordinary case when privately asserted claims or publicly asserted demands are being resisted, or when it is being contended that procedures or means should be provided to support rights. Rights make their most important appearances at the stage when one is attempting to back up a claim or assert a new claim: we argue for these (in part) by appealing to rights. Of course we do not always talk as if this is the central role of rights, and there may be little need to do so; but this way of looking at rights has two virtues. It accounts for some phenomena that the alternative view does not account for; and it is a fruitful way of looking at rights in that, as in the holder in due course problem, it illuminates distinctions of social importance, and, as in the privacy issue, where we find a right largely unprotected, it indicates directions in which to move.

If the character of legal rights derives from the foregoing, what *is* their character? Rights are essentially counters deployed in legal argument; and they are strong counters: they have weight and ought to be treated accordingly by legal decision-makers. This seems to me to be a necessary feature of legal rights, but it is not sufficient, for there are other weighty counters in legal argument—for example, those connected with social welfare—that do not (necessarily) give one rights. Legal rights are weighty counters that have to do with one's self, one's person, one's personality, one's individuality. I think that the integrity of one's self is a part of it, and here I include one's physical and mental integrity, and also one's reputation, which might be called one's social integrity. I would also include one's sense of self-esteem.

So far this characterization seems adequate for many of the rights that we have been considering—general rights like the rights to privacy, personal security, and free speech. What of property rights? Such rights are in part special rights, but with some hesitation I suggest that they can also be fit into the framework just outlined. Property owners (or at least the owners of certain kinds of property) usually have expectations having to do with their security, status, the kinds of futures they are likely to have, and related matters, and these expectations are legitimate in the sense that they are formed as a result of actions that are legal. Certain ways of disappointing these expectations are likely to be detrimental to a person, not unlike the ways in which stealing is detrimental to a person, and so protection of these expectations is needed in order to protect the self. If this suggestion is at all illuminating for property rights, what of special rights such as contractual rights? It is possible, I think, to view in the same light the position of one who has been disappointed by a breach of contract. I am somewhat hesitant about suggesting this, since in the case of rights arising out of contractual relations it seems to be the agreement itself, not the integrity of the contracting parties, that is central to the right. But the category of special rights is not limited to rights arising out of mutual voluntary undertakings. The rights of parents and children against one another rest on a relation that is not one of mutual voluntary undertakings, and I do not see the impetus for ascribing rights to a child merely on the basis of its status as a child unless this has to do with something about the child itself—its self, integrity, and the rest. It should be noted, in support of this, that though in our legal system many of the child's rights are protected by claims against the parent, there are legal systems in which these rights are supported by claims against institutions established for this purpose, and there are other, less formal social systems in which a child's rights are supported by claims against other members of the family.

Though the character of legal rights derives from their most important roles—in legal decision-making where one is attempting to back up a claim or assert a new claim—rights are by no means the only counters in decision-making, nor even always the principal consideration. Rights can of course be outweighed by other rights—even by less important ones if these are much more seriously threatened in a particular case. But rights—even important ones—can also be overridden in order to prevent disaster; for example, important political rights might be suspended in time of emergency. And rights can sometimes be outweighed by important social and economic policies; for example, the policy of discouraging monopolization might sometimes outweigh the right to enter freely into contracts.* But if rights are not always the weightiest consideration, they are of special importance, as evidenced by the fact that reasons of welfare and of policy must be especially weighty in order to override them. Not just any desirable end is more important than the interests protected as rights.

* This can happen in connection with what are called covenants not to compete, in which an employee agrees not to enter into a business or employment in competition with his employer after termination of the employment for a specified period of time and within a specified area.

Notes

Notes

Chapter One

1. Sir William Blackstone, *Commentaries on the Laws of England,* 16th ed. (London, 1825), 1: 41.

2. Jeremy Bentham, *A Comment on the Commentaries: A Criticism of William Blackstone's Commentaries on the Laws of England,* ed. Charles Warren Everett (Oxford, Eng., 1928), pp. 213–14.

3. Jerome Frank, *Law and the Modern Mind* (Garden City, N.Y., 1963), pp. 46–49. In a footnote Frank says that the questions involved in this example "are very nearly those involved in *Black & White Taxi & T. Co. v. Brown & Yellow Taxi & T. Co.,* 276 U.S. 518."

4. Joseph C. Hutcheson, Jr., "The Judgment Intuitive: The Function of the 'Hunch' in Judicial Decision," *Cornell Law Quarterly,* 14 (1928): 279.

5. Frank, p. 125. See also Karl Llewellyn, "Some Realism About Realism," *Harvard Law Review,* 44 (1931): 1253.

6. Frank, p. 144. Italics in original.

7. John Chipman Gray, *The Nature and Sources of the Law* (Boston, 1963).

8. *Ibid.,* p. 84.

9. *Ibid.,* p. 101.

10. *Ibid.,* pp. 124–25.

11. *Ibid.,* p. 170. Italics in original.

12. *Ibid.,* pp. 102, 125, 172. Italics in original.

13. *Ibid.,* p. 102.

14. *Ibid.,* p. 100.

15. *Ibid.*

16. *Ibid.*

17. *Ibid.,* p. 84.

18. *Ibid.,* p. 101.

19. *Ibid.,* p. 124.

20. *Ibid.,* pp. 267–68.

21. *Ibid.,* p. 234.

22. *Ibid.,* pp. 143–44, 309.

23. *Ibid.*, p. 290. See, in contrast, Patrick Devlin, "Morals and the Criminal Law," in his *The Enforcement of Morals* (London, 1968). See also Ronald Dworkin's criticism of Devlin on this point in "Lord Devlin and the Enforcement of Morals," in Richard Wasserstrom, ed., *Morality and the Law* (Belmont, Calif., 1971).

24. Gray, *Nature and Sources*, p. 89. Gray is here arguing against John Austin's view of the relation between law and sovereign.

25. *Ibid.*, pp. 65, 69, 103.   26. *Ibid.*, p. 79.

27. *Ibid.*, p. 103.   28. *Ibid.*, p. 121.

29. *Ibid.*, p. 123.   30. *Ibid.*, p. 122.

31. *Ibid.*

32. Frank, *Law and Modern Mind*, p. 133.

33. *Ibid.*, pp. 132–33. Italics in original.

34. *Ibid.*, Chap. 16. On the general verdict, see Mortimer R. Kadish and Sanford H. Kadish, *Discretion to Disobey* (Stanford, Calif., 1973), pp. 45ff.

35. Joseph W. Bingham, "What Is the Law?," *Michigan Law Review*, 11 (1912).

36. Oliver Wendell Holmes, "The Path of the Law," in *Collected Legal Papers* (New York, 1921), p. 173.

37. Oliver Wendell Holmes, *The Common Law* (Cambridge, Mass., 1963), p. 5.

38. Edgar Bodenheimer, *Jurisprudence* (1962), p. 115, quoted in John D. Finch, *Introduction to Legal Theory* (London, 1970), p. 137.

39. Holmes, "Path of the Law," pp. 171, 173.

40. H. L. A. Hart, *The Concept of Law* (Oxford, Eng., 1961), p. 43.

41. Frank, *Law and Modern Mind*, pp. 50–51.

42. *Ibid.*, p. 56.

43. Richard Taylor, "Law and Morality," *New York University Law Review*, 43 (1968): 627. Italics in original.

44. 115 N.Y. 506, 22 N.E. 188 (1889). This case is often used as an example and will come up again later.

45. Taylor, p. 626. Italics in original.

46. *Ibid.*, p. 634.

47. Felix S. Cohen. "Transcendental Nonsense and the Functional Approach," *Columbia Law Review*, 35 (1935): 813–14. Italics in original.

48. Llewellyn, "Some Realism," pp. 1252–53.

49. See, for example, Roscoe Pound, *Social Control Through Law* (New Haven, Conn., 1942); quotations from Pound will appear a bit further on.

50. George C. Christie, *Jurisprudence* (St. Paul, Minn., 1973), p. 751.

51. Frank, *Law and Modern Mind*, p. 112.

52. Llewellyn, p. 1244.

53. 347 U.S. 483, 494, 74 S.Ct. 686, 692–93.

54. Pound, pp. 65, 109–10.

55. Roscoe Pound, "A Survey of Social Interests," *Harvard Law Review*, 57 (1943); and "A Survey of Public Interests," *Harvard Law Review*, 58 (1945).

56. Pound, "Social Interests," pp. 16–17.

57. Karl Llewellyn, "A Realistic Jurisprudence–the Next Step," *Columbia Law Review*, 30 (1930): p. 435n.

58. These problems are taken up in Theodore M. Benditt, "Law and the Balancing of Interests," *Social Theory and Practice*, 3 (1975). See also Charles Fried, "Two Concepts of Interests: Some Reflections on the Supreme Court's Balancing Test," *Harvard Law Review*, 76 (1963).

59. Lord Radcliffe, *The Law and Its Compass* (1960), p. 16, quoted in Louis L. Jaffe, *English and American Judges as Lawmakers* (Oxford, Eng., 1969), pp. 7–8. See also Paul J. Mishkin, "Foreword: The 1964 Supreme Court Term," *Harvard Law Review*, 79 (1965): 62–70.

Chapter Two

1. Oliver Wendell Holmes, *The Common Law* (Cambridge, Mass., 1963), p. 1.

2. Holmes's dissenting opinion in Southern Pacific Co. v. Jensen, 244 U.S. 205, 222 (1917).

3. Alf Ross, *Towards a Realistic Jurisprudence* (1946), quoted in John Passmore, "Hagerstrom's Philosophy of Law," *Philosophy*, 36 (1961): 145.

4. See Passmore's article cited in the preceding note.

5. Karl Llewellyn, "A Realistic Jurisprudence–the Next Step," *Columbia Law Review*, 30 (1930): especially pp. 439ff.

6. Joseph W. Bingham, "What Is the Law?," *Michigan Law Review*, 11 (1912), quoted in M. Golding, *The Nature of Law* (New York, 1966), pp. 216–17.

7. This point is discussed at length by H. L. A. Hart in *The Concept of Law* (Oxford, Eng., 1961), pp. 138ff.

8. *Ibid.*, p. 141.

9. See, e.g., George C. Christie, "Objectivity in the Law," *Yale Law Journal*, 78 (1969): 1314.

10. Hart, p. 125.

11. Hart, p. 119.

12. *Ibid.*

13. It is a "mistake . . . to assume that, because a judge has decided a case in accordance with a general rule, the rule must have existed

before the case came into court" (John Chipman Gray, *The Nature and Sources of the Law*, Boston, Mass., 1963, p. 230).

14. Ronald Dworkin, "The Model of Rules," *University of Chicago Law Review*, 35 (1967): 32, 33. (Reprinted as "Is Law a System of Rules?," in R. S. Summers, ed., *Essays in Legal Philosophy*, Berkeley, Calif., 1968.)

15. See R. M. Hare, *The Language of Morals* (New York, 1964), pp. 6off, 71ff; and Hart, *Concept of Law*, pp. 121–22.

16. See A. W. B. Simpson, "The Common Law and Legal Theory," in A. W. B. Simpson, ed., *Oxford Essays in Jurisprudence* (2d series; Oxford, Eng., 1973), who suggests that to think of rules of law is to think of a precise, detailed code of law.

17. Christie, "Objectivity in the Law," p. 1320.

18. See Hart, *Concept of Law*, p. 123; and John Dickinson, "Legal Rules: Their Function in the Process of Decision," *University of Pennsylvania Law Review*, 79 (1931): 846–47.

19. See Ronald Dworkin, "A Theory of Civil Disobedience," in Howard E. Kiefer and Milton K. Munitz, eds., *Ethics and Social Justice* (Albany, N.Y., 1968), pp. 234–35.

20. This is how I interpret Christie, "Objectivity in the Law," pp. 1314, 1316, 1319.

21. Karl Llewellyn, "Some Realism About Realism," *Harvard Law Review*, 44 (1931): 1237.

Chapter Three

1. For example, Richard Wasserstrom, *The Judicial Decision* (Stanford, Calif., 1961).

2. For example, Kenneth Culp Davis, *Discretionary Justice* (Urbana, Ill., 1971).

3. Wolfgang Friedmann, *Legal Theory* (5th ed.; London, 1967), pp. 274, 287.

4. Donald J. Black, "The Boundaries of Legal Sociology," *Yale Law Journal*, 81 (1972): 1087.

5. *Ibid.*, pp. 1089, 1096.

6. Geoffrey Sawer, *Law in Society* (Oxford, Eng., 1965), p. 9. See also Alf Ross, *On Law and Justice* (Berkeley, Calif., 1958), pp. 19–24.

7. Oliver Wendell Holmes, "The Path of the Law," in *Collected Legal Papers* (New York, 1921), p. 173; Jerome Frank, *Law and the Modern Mind* (Garden City, N.Y., 1963), p. 51. Italics in original.

8. Maurice Mandelbaum, "Societal Facts," *The British Journal of Sociology*, 6 (1955), p. 307.

9. *Ibid.*, pp. 307, 312. See also Mandelbaum's "Psychology and

Societal Facts," in Robert Colodny, ed., *Logic, Laws, and Life* (Pittsburgh, 1977).

10. Alf Ross, *On Law*, pp. 13–14.

11. Alf Ross, *Directives and Norms* (London, 1968), p. 35.

12. *Ibid.*

13. H. L. A. Hart, *The Concept of Law* (Oxford, Eng., 1961), pp. 55–56, 88.

14. The discussion in the next two pages has benefited from Marshall Cohen's paper "Law and Force" (unpublished). See also Robert Nozick, *Anarchy, State, and Utopia* (New York, 1974), p. 23.

15. Ross, *On Law*, p. 59. See also pp. 34, 52ff.

16. Hans Kelsen, *General Theory of Law and State*, tr. Anders Wedberg (Cambridge, Mass., 1945), p. 29.

17. This view is held by Joseph Raz ("The Identity of Legal Systems," *California Law Review*, 59 [1971]: 802–3), who brings out many of its limitations. See also A. M. Honoré, "Groups, Laws, and Obedience," in A. W. B. Simpson, ed., *Oxford Essays in Jurisprudence*, (2d series; Oxford, Eng., 1973).

18. Honoré, p. 1.

19. H. L. A. Hart, *Definition and Theory in Jurisprudence*, Inaugural Lecture, Oxford University (London, 1953), p. 7. (Reprinted in *The Law Quarterly Review*, Jan. 1954.)

20. Jonathan Cohen, "Theory and Definition in Jurisprudence," *Proceedings of the Aristotelian Society*, Supplement, 1955.

21. Hart, "Definition," p. 16.

Chapter Four

1. John Austin, *The Province of Jurisprudence Determined* (London, 1968), p. 18. Italics in original.

2. But see Richard Taylor, "Law and Morality," *New York University Law Review*, 43 (1968).

3. Most of these points are found in H. L. A. Hart, *The Concept of Law* (Oxford, Eng., 1961), pp. 18–25, 49ff, 81.

4. Hans Kelsen makes such a move in *General Theory of Law and State*, tr. Anders Wedberg (Cambridge, Mass., 1945), pp. 62–64. Marshall Cohen, in "Law and Force" (unpublished paper), has pointed out that such a move is equally available to Austin.

5. See also Taylor, pp. 646–47.

6. Hart, p. 83.

7. See Rolf Sartorious, "The Concept of Law," *Archives for Philosophy of Law and Social Philosophy*, 53 (1967).

8. Hart, pp. 89–90.

9. See Joseph Raz, "The Identity of Legal Systems," *California Law Review,* 59 (1971).

10. Hart, *Concept of Law,* p. 246.

11. *Ibid.,* p. 107.

12. 1 Cranch 137 (1803).

13. Hart, p. 149.

14. Hart, pp. 64–69, 103.

15. Ronald Dworkin, "The Model of Rules," *University of Chicago Law Review,* 35 (1967): 22. (Reprinted as "Is Law a System of Rules?," in R. S. Summers, ed., *Essays in Legal Philosophy,* Berkeley, Calif., 1968.)

16. This quote and the ones that follow appear on pp. 23 and 25–27 of the journal article. (See preceding note.)

17. 115 N.Y. 506, 511, 22 N.E. 188, 190 (1889).

18. Compare Hart's related problem with custom, in Dworkin, "Model of Rules," pp. 42–44.

19. *Ibid.,* p. 37.

20. *Ibid.,* p. 38.

21. *Ibid.,* p. 33.

22. Ronald Dworkin, "Social Rules and Legal Theory," *Yale Law Journal,* 81 (1972): 881.

23. Dworkin, "Model of Rules," pp. 30–31, and "Social Rules," pp. 879ff. See also his "Philosophy and the Critique of Law," in Robert Paul Wolff, ed., *The Rule of Law* (New York, 1971).

24. Ronald Dworkin, "Law and Civil Disobedience," in James Rachels, ed., *Moral Problems* (New York, 1971), p. 152.

25. Dworkin, "Model of Rules," p. 40.

26. Dworkin, "Social Rules," pp. 857–58.

27. *Ibid.,* pp. 862–63.

28. See Joseph Raz, "Legal Principles and the Limits of Law," *Yale Law Journal,* 81 (1972): 851–54.

Chapter Five

1. This topic is also taken up by Thomas Morawetz, "The Rules of Law and the Point of Law," *University of Pennsylvania Law Review,* 121 (1973).

2. Thomas Aquinas, *Summa Theologiae,* I-II, q. 94, a.2.

3. Henningsen v. Bloomfield Motors, Inc., 32 N.J. 358, at 389, 161 A. 2d 69, at 86 (1960).

4. H. L. A. Hart, *The Concept of Law* (Oxford, Eng., 1961), pp. 194n, 195.

5. Lon L. Fuller, *The Morality of Law* (New Haven, Conn., 1964), p. 106. See also p. 96 and elsewhere.

6. *Ibid.*, p. 39.

7. *Ibid.*

8. See *ibid.*, p. 96.

9. This possibility is considered by Ronald Dworkin, "The Elusive Morality of Law," *Villanova Law Review*, 10 (1965): 632; and by David Lyons, "The Internal Morality of Law," *Proceedings of the Aristotelian Society*, 71 (1971). Some of the points that follow are made in these articles.

10. Lon L. Fuller, "Human Purpose and Natural Law," *Journal of Philosophy*, 53 (1956); reprinted in *Natural Law Forum*, 3 (1958). Some of the remarks that follow come from Ernest Nagel, "Fact, Value, and Human Purpose," *Natural Law Forum*, 4 (1959); and from Marshall Cohen, "Law, Morality and Purpose," *Villanova Law Review*, 10 (1965).

11. R. M. Hare, *The Language of Morals* (New York, 1964), p. 100. In this and the next two paragraphs I borrow from Hare, pp. 100–101.

12. For related remarks, see A. V. Cragg, "Functional Words, Facts and Values," *Canadian Journal of Philosophy*, 6 (1976): 85.

13. R. M. Hare, "Geach: Good and Evil," in Philippa Foot, ed., *Theories of Ethics* (Oxford, Eng., 1967), pp. 79–80.

14. Hart, *Concept of Law*, p. 113.

15. *Ibid.*, p. 114.

16. A similar point is made by Kurt Baier in "Obligation: Political and Moral," in J. Roland Pennock and John W. Chapman, eds., *Nomos XII: Political and Legal Obligation* (New York, 1970), pp. 124–25.

17. There is much on this in John Rawls's *A Theory of Justice* (Cambridge, Mass., 1971), though his contribution to this topic has not yet received much attention in the critical literature.

18. On this point, see Ronald Dworkin, "Law and Civil Disobedience," in James Rachels, ed., *Moral Problems* (New York, 1971), pp. 145–53.

19. Hare, "Geach," p. 82n.

20. As discussed in Chap. 2. See Rolf Sartorious, "Social Policy and Judicial Legislation," *American Philosophical Quarterly*, 8 (1971): 156–59.

Chapter Six

1. John Austin, *The Province of Jurisprudence Determined* (London, 1968), pp. 17–18. Italics in original.

2. Richard Taylor, "Law and Morality," *New York University Law Review*, 43 (1968): 646. Italics in original.

3. H. L. A. Hart, *The Concept of Law* (Oxford, Eng., 1961), p. 83.

4. *Ibid.*, pp. 84, 85.

5. *Ibid.*, p. 82.

6. Kurt Baier, "Moral Obligation," *American Philosophical Quarterly*, 3 (1966): 216.

7. See John R. Searle, "How to Derive 'Ought' from 'Is'," *Philosophical Review*, 73 (1964). There is an extensive literature on this topic. See W. D. Hudson, ed., *The Is/Ought Question* (London, 1969). Searle replies to objections in his book *Speech Acts* (Cambridge, Eng., 1970), Chap. 8. Some of his replies involve slight modifications in the argument that do not affect the present discussion.

8. See, for example, Robert Paul Wolff, *In Defense of Anarchism* (New York, 1970); and John Ladd, "Legal and Moral Obligation," in J. Roland Pennock and John W. Chapman, eds., *Nomos XII: Political and Legal Obligation* (New York, 1970).

9. For a statement of a rule utilitarian theory, see R. B. Brandt, "Toward a Credible Form of Utilitarianism," in H.-N. Casteñeda and G. Nakhnikian, eds., *Morality and the Language of Conduct* (Detroit, 1965). See David Lyons, *In the Interest of the Governed* (Oxford, Eng., 1973), pp. 45ff, for a discussion of Bentham's views.

10. 394 U.S. 147, 151 (1969). See also Women Strike for Peace v. Hickel, 420 F. 2d 597, 606 (D.C. Cir., 1969); and Strasser v. Doorley, 432 F. 2d 567, 568 (1st Cir., 1970).

11. Dissent in Jones v. Opelika, 316 U.S. 584, 602, adopted *per curiam* on rehearing, 319 U.S. 103, 104 (1943). The point is also made quite clearly in Strasser v. Doorley, 432 F. 2d 567, 568 (1st Cir., 1970), citing Shuttlesworth: "And clearly where, as will appear in the case here, we hold the ordinance unconstitutional on its face, there can be no question of the plaintiff's standing [to raise the constitutional question in his defense]."

12. This position appears to be taken by Kurt Baier in both "Moral Obligation," p. 217, and "Obligation: Political and Moral," in Pennock and Chapman, eds., *Nomos XII*, pp. 133–34.

13. This is the view of R. B. Brandt in "Utility and the Obligation to Obey the Law," in Sidney Hook, ed., *Law and Philosophy* (New York, 1964), pp. 46–47.

14. Hart replies in this way to Gustav Radbruch in "Legal Positivism and the Separation of Law and Morals," *Harvard Law Review*, 71 (1958), part 4.

15. Brandt, "Utility," p. 51.

16. *Ibid.* Italics in original.

17. See Laurent B. Frantz, "The First Amendment in the Balance," *Yale Law Journal*, 71 (1962); and Charles Fried, "Two Concepts of Interests: Some Reflections on the Supreme Court's Balancing Test," *Harvard Law Review*, 76 (1963).

Chapter Seven

1. Hans Oberdiek, "The Role of Sanctions and Coercion in Understanding Law and Legal Systems," *American Journal of Jurisprudence*, 21 (1976).

2. H. L. A. Hart, *The Concept of Law* (Oxford, Eng., 1961), pp. 33–35.

3. Philip Mullock, "Nullity and Sanction," *Mind*, 83 (1974): 439–41.

4. Minder v. Minder, 83 N.J.Super. 159, 199 A.2d 69, at 71 (1964).

5. Landsman v. Landsman, 302 N.Y. 45, 96 N.E.2d 81 (1950); Johnson County National Bank & Trust Company v. Bach, 189 Kan. 291, 369 P.2d 231 (Sup. Ct., 1962); Minder v. Minder, as cited in the preceding note.

6. Hart, *Concept*, p. 34.

7. Mullock, p. 441, finally rejects the view that there is no difference between nullity and sanction, for reasons similar to these.

8. John Stuart Mill, *On Liberty*, ed. Currin V. Shields (Indianapolis, 1956), pp. 94–95.

9. Oliver Wendell Holmes, "The Path of the Law," in *Collected Legal Papers* (New York, 1921), p. 175.

10. Sir William Blackstone, *Commentaries on the Laws of England*, 16th ed. (London, 1825), 1: 58.

11. See pp. 102–3, above.

12. Oberdiek, "Role of Sanctions," p. 93. Italics in original.

13. *Ibid.*, p. 94.

14. Norberto Bobbio, "The Promotion of Action in the Modern State," in Graham Hughes, ed., *Law, Reason, and Justice* (New York, 1969), pp. 202, 203.

15. *Ibid.*, pp. 191–92.

Chapter Eight

1. Wesley N. Hohfeld, *Fundamental Legal Conceptions as Applied in Judicial Reasoning*, ed. W. W. Cook (New Haven, Conn., 1964), p. 35.

2. *Ibid.*

3. *Ibid.*, p. 36.

4. Glanville Williams, "The Concept of Legal Liberty," in R. S. Summers, ed., *Essays in Legal Philosophy* (Berkeley, Calif., 1968), pp. 131–32.

5. Arthur L. Corbin, "Legal Analysis and Terminology," *Yale Law Journal*, 29 (1919): 165.

6. Hohfeld, p. 75.

7. *Ibid.*, p. 72. Italics in original.

8. See Joel Feinberg, "Duties, Rights, and Claims," *American Philosophical Quarterly*, 3 (1966): 141–42.

9. David Lyons, "Rights, Claimants, and Beneficiaries," *American Philosophical Quarterly*, 6 (1969): 176.

10. H. L. A. Hart, "Bentham on Legal Rights," in A. W. B. Simpson, ed., *Oxford Essays in Jurisprudence* (2d series; Oxford, Eng., 1973), p. 190.

11. John Chipman Gray, *The Nature and Sources of the Law* (Boston, 1963), p. 19.

12. David Braybrooke, "The Firm But Untidy Correlativity of Rights and Obligations," *Canadian Journal of Philosophy*, 1 (1972).

13. See Griswold v. Connecticut, 381 U.S. 479, 85 S.Ct. 1678 (1965).

14. See William L. Prosser, *Handbook of the Law of Torts*, 4th ed. (St. Paul, Minn., 1971), p. 816. See also Nader v. General Motors Corp. (1968), 292 N.Y.S.2d 514 (damages); and Galella v. Onassis (1972), 353 F.Supp. 196, 231–32 (injunction and civil contempt).

15. This distinction is drawn by Ronald Dworkin in "The Model of Rules," *University of Chicago Law Review*, 35 (1967). See also his "Social Rules and Legal Theory," *Yale Law Journal*, 81 (1972).

16. See Joseph Raz, "Legal Principles and the Limits of Law," *Yale Law Journal*, 81 (1972): 827–29.

17. See Samuel D. Warren and Louis D. Brandeis, "The Right to Privacy," *Harvard Law Review*, 4 (1890).

18. This argument is given by A. M. Honoré in "Rights of Exclusion and Immunities Against Divesting," *Tulane Law Review*, 34 (1960): 456–57.

19. *Ibid.*, pp. 461ff.

Index

Index